The Psychic and the Detective

INNER VISIONS SERIES #3

The Psychic and the Detective

Ann Druffel with **Armand Marcotte**

This book is dedicated to

Ellen R. Mary Druffel, Ph.D.
who loves earth's mysteries

and to

Irene Dumont
a beautiful mother

International Standard Book Number 0-917086-53-8

Cover Design by Larry Ortiz

Printed in the United States of America

Published by ACS Publications, Inc.
P.O. Box 16430
San Diego, CA 92116-0430

TABLE OF CONTENTS

ACKNOWLEDGMENTS

Many persons helped the authors during the preparation of this book. We wish to give special thanks to the wonderful detectives who have sought Armand Marcotte's help and to Dwane Bass, who helps organize and coordinate Armand's appointments.

We owe special thanks to Louise Ludwig, Ph.D., for her invaluable advice and counsel, and to our publisher, Neil F. Michelson. Our appreciation goes out to the following persons who read parts of this manuscript and offered advice and suggestions: Stephan A. Schwartz, Alice Nordstrom, Helevei Nordstrom, and Dorothy Shapiro. Last, but never least, thanks to Marjorie and Raymond Bayless, Norma and Hamilton Farmer, and Berthold E. Schwarz, M.D., for unfailing moral support and friendship.

AUTHORS' NOTE: Jack Webb said it first, "The names have been changed to protect the innocent." For the same reason, the names of victims, detectives and cities concerned with the crimes discussed in this book have been changed.

Armand Marcotte works with detectives under a code of strict confidentiality, but we are free to use the four cases in this book because they received publicity in various local newspapers. We will use pseudonyms, nevertheless, to protect those involved from unwelcome publicity. Verification of facts and actual names involved are in the files of the authors.

INTRODUCTION

This is not a scientific book. It neither pretends to be nor is it intended to be. But it is a true book in that it is based, as far as humanly possible, on verified material, and the attitude with which it is written is objective, questioning and careful.

It is written for one purpose — to demonstrate that psychic detective teamwork, properly employed, could solve many of the problems which law enforcement officials and the society they serve are facing today.

This book is not intended as a thick, scholarly tome. We have deliberately avoided pedanticism and statistical graphs. Instead, we have attempted to press human beings within its pages — human beings with all their emotions, problems and individual philosophies of life. Our sincere hope is that the reader can bring these human beings to life and learn how the budding science of psychic/detective interaction can aid in this era of exploding crime, deflated police budgets and deterioration of social mores.

There are all types of psychics. They come in differing sizes, shapes, colors and manner of dress. They are not alike as peas but as different as lima beans and cabbages. Some wear jeans, others business suits. Some are broad, strong and comfortable. Others are shy, wispy and spiritual. Some are as earthy as our mother planet herself and outspoken to unpleasant degrees; others are mild-mannered and mold themselves to situations with obliging smiles.

Detectives, too, come in differing appearances, each as individual as nature can make them. How do these two types of persons — detectives and psychics — accommodate themselves to each other in the chancy association known as detective/psychic teamwork? There is only one solid answer at present: with difficulty!

Often the detectives cannot understand how the psychics work. They regard them as strange, erratic and difficult to relate to. They do not know whether to act believing or skeptical toward the information psychics are offering. On the other hand, psychics have trouble relating to detectives. They subconsciously wonder why they are used only as a last resort, when earlier contact might have strengthened their input in the investigation of violent crimes.

Psychics have difficulty expressing the intuitional material they receive in terms that scientifically-trained police can understand. They do not know how to "train" detectives when to keep silent and when to ask questions during the time psychic information is flowing from their minds.

This book might be regarded as (and we hope it may prove to be) a readable, entertaining preliminary "training manual" for both psychics **and** detectives, and also for all those citizens who are interested in this subject. It explains in detail how one psychic, Armand Marcotte of Fontana California, thinks, feels and works. Hopefully, by providing this understanding of how **one** clairvoyant has conquered the vagaries of detective/psychic teamwork, others will be encouraged to conquer them also.

We have attempted to include sound tips on how productive relationships can be set up between other detectives and other psychics. Some facets of this work can be set down as general rules, but for the most part such working relationships are as individual as the persons themselves. Mutual knowledge of each other's limitations, mutual tolerance for each other's frailties and mutual respect for each other's talents will produce successful teams.

Above all, the detective/psychic team must be regarded as a partnership — albeit a temporary one. Mutual charity, blended with all-absorbing desire to solve violent crimes, are the keys.

Ann Druffel
Armand Marcotte

CHAPTER ONE

"The Beginning"

Armand Marcotte unlocked the door of his office and stepped inside. Turning on the lights to banish the gloom of a rainy Friday, he slipped out of his rain-spattered coat and pulled a favorite old sweater over his head. For a summer day in California the chill was unusual. Sitting at his desk, he pondered how his recent decision could make his life more orderly and relaxed.

Outside his office the increasing murmur of voices — cosmetologists, students and clients — failed to penetrate his consciousness. For Armand had the ability to block out anything he didn't want to hear or think or see.

He'd decided at last to sell the school, for the cosmetology school in Upland and the growing business from his trailer office in Fontana were too much to manage.

He liked teaching and needed a relaxing atmosphere to work in. That was the reason he'd first established the school, which he had puckishly named "Armand's Hair Safari." His students were bright and dedicated and his clientele happy. It had been a satisfying fifteen years.

But the triangle he traveled each day was **not** relaxing — from his home in Hesperia deep in the desert far east of Los Angeles; to Upland, the westernmost point of the triad; to Fontana, which lay on the flatlands just east of the mountain rim of the Los Angeles Basin; and back again to Hesperia.

Armand felt a familiar pull — the clients outside who subconsciously wanted him to come out and "tell them things." Some of his clients came to his shop because they liked his students' work. Others came because they liked him as a person. But others, he knew, came only in the hope of picking up a word of advice, or a stray perception he might wish to share, regarding some important event he saw coming toward them in time. It was this last group that were really bugging him. They had eventually forced him into the difficult decision to put his school up for sale. The date was September 15, 1978.

He'd miss the teaching, for in spite of the fact Armand had only a few years of formal education, he was a natural teacher — patient, soft-voiced and kind. But he had a way of **knowing** what each student needed to succeed and did not hesitate to speak forcefully at times if it was necessary to put his point across.

Most people liked him for his many talents and easy personality, but Armand still felt, as he had always felt since he was a small child that he didn't really have many true friends.

As a child he had always been treated by other children and adults as though he were different, for the natural clairvoyance which was an essential part of his personality dismayed and frightened others.

He'd learned to quell the psychic impressions as he grew to adulthood, so that he could turn them on and off almost at will, but his natural desire to help people (whom he regarded as his brothers and sisters under a loving Father) had prompted him to tell people he liked bits of information he perceived psychically about them. He tried to limit these informal readings to information which would help them make important life decisions, steer them away from danger or assist in solving other personal problems.

It had been this way with the clients and students at his cosmetology school. He had favorite people he shared things with, of course, but never spoke out in clairvoyant terms to any customers who would be scared away. He was always careful to withhold information if he felt the person involved was not ready for it.

Now, on this gloomy Friday, Valerie Montes rapped twice on the door, opened it quickly and poked in her curly head.

"Can I clean your office now, Armand?" she inquired. "I've got some important telephone calls to make. Want to hurry up a little so I can do your trailer today, too."

"Sure," responded Armand obligingly. "Just work around me."

"I called my mother today already," said Valerie, as she began to dust the furniture. "I should have done it days ago, but you know how it is. You put things off, and then all of a sudden you decide you've simply **got** to straighten things out that are wrong."

Armand nodded automatically, relaxing at last from the pain of his decision to sell. Suddenly, glancing at Valerie, he involuntarily slipped into the gray twilight zone that signaled his travels into clairvoyant perceptions. He saw a vision of Valerie, bloody and mutilated in a woody area.

Startled, Armand tried to push the image away, but it was far too strong. He slipped again into the grayness and found himself on a time track of his cleaning woman's life. What he saw in her immediate future was so devastating that he pushed his way out and found himself staring at Valerie who was very much alive. She was vacuuming the carpet, happily humming a mariachi tune.

"Valerie," ventured Armand. "I see so much danger around you this weekend. Whatever you do, **don't** leave your house tonight! Because if you do, I don't see you returning!"

Valerie stopped working, stared at him a second, and then broke into a merry laugh. Rita, one of Armand's students, happened to be walking by the open door. She **didn't** laugh.

"Don't **say** that, Armand!" Rita exclaimed. "You scare me!"

"I'm telling **Valerie**," replied Armand. "I see you having an argument, Valerie, and walking out of your home."

"So?" countered Valerie, and she pushed the vacuum cleaner toward the other side of the small room.

Armand thought quickly. Only twice in his life had he received perceptions of such violence around persons he knew well. Usually such clairvoyant knowledge came when he sought it deliberately in his Fontana trailer office. But remembering his impressions regarding Raymond, a homeless stray he'd taken in and whom he kiddingly called his "son," he decided that these remarkably clear impressions should not be ignored.

"Valerie," Armand insisted. "Stay home tonight! Even if you don't **want** to. I see you getting in a car and **not coming back**! They'll arrest your husband —"

Armand looked into Valerie's skeptical face and fought with his conscience. Should he tell her **all** he'd seen? Valerie having a violent argument with her husband — Valerie, stomping out of the house, then using the public telephone at a corner call box. Then, three young men driving up in a car, one getting out and leaving the group. Then the two who were left calling to Valerie and inviting her in.

Worst of all, Armand perceived that the two had been drinking or were stoned on drugs. Then the horrible sight of Valerie's butchered body lying in a wooded area, perhaps a park, victim of a sadistic murder.

He heard Valerie laughing at him. "Oh, Armand. Don't be that way. You're working too much with these policemen lately. You've got to cut it out." And she turned back to her work, hurried but efficient, doing her cleaning chores twice as well, in half the time, as any other cleaning person Armand had ever hired before.

Armand decided to stop. After all, when he was talked back to like that, what was the use of trying to force his opinion? And, of course, there was always the chance that **he** might be wrong —

The day wore on and Valerie finished her work quickly, as usual. She stopped by Armand's office for her pay. She charged $6.00 an hour, almost twice what other women got for day work at that time, but Armand always knew she was worth every dime.

He had wondered, when she first began working for him, why such a beautiful, talented young person would be seeking employment as a cleaning person.

"Armand," she had replied. "I can make more money this way than as a waitress or a secretary. I don't waste time and effort, and you can always count on me."

Armand soon found that all this was true. Valerie was reliable and competent, and he'd hired her to clean not only Armand's Hair Safari but his Hesperia mobile home and his Fontana office as well.

Now on this fateful Friday, Armand paid Valerie her week's wages. Delightedly, she withdrew a small package from her large purse and showed the contents to him. They were nicely made-up business cards which stated in firm block letters, "Valerie Montes — Cleaning Service," and her telephone number.

"Now I'm really in business, Armand. What do you think? Classy! Business cards and all!"

Armand complimented her on her good taste, but his mind wasn't on the cards. He was still thinking about the horrifying vision that had burst upon his consciousness — Valerie lying dead and bloodied on green grass, the night wind stirring softly through tall trees.

"I wish you wouldn't go out, though, Valerie," Armand tried again. "I'm really worried." Should he tell her about the three young men in the car, and the fact he'd seen one getting out because he didn't want to have anything to do with what the other two were planning? He started again to warn her about the fearful consequences if she went out that evening.

Valerie again shrugged off the warning, bid Armand a cheery "Adios," and left to clean his Fontana office.

Armand finished out the day, deliberately quelling his anxiety about Valerie. At the very edge of his conscious mind, he sometimes wondered whether or not his precognitive visions were simply events coming forward in time, or if he, somehow, helped **cause** these happenings. Subconsciously, this unquiet feeling knocked now at his mental door; he put the whole thing out of his mind, determined to enjoy the weekend and trusting that Valerie would take his advice.

That evening after the summer thundershower subsided, the California heat took hold again. The air was heavy with humidity — the kind of weather that makes tempers soar.

Valerie's mood was bad. She'd finished her work at Armand's office but had absentmindedly left her package of new business cards there and realized she wouldn't have the pleasure of showing them to her family that night. Other little things also went wrong as the evening progressed, and soon Valerie was having a violent argument with her husband, Carlos. Leaving him and her pretty little daughter, she stormed out of the house, determined to have fun without them.

She drove rapidly to a nearby store and used the outside telephone booth to call a girlfriend. She made tentative plans for her chum to meet her on the corner.

Something happened — her friend didn't appear at the appointed time. Valerie waited impatiently, still angry at Carlos. She kept hoping he wouldn't come out looking for her and force her to come home with him.

Waiting was alien to Valerie. She was used to doing everything efficiently and on time, or ahead of time. Competence and haste were the contradictory keystones of her philosophy.

She saw a car pull up near the phone booth. Three young men were inside, and Valerie recognized one of them. From their behavior Valerie realized they'd been doing **something** to have a good time; maybe someone had given them some freebee drugs. They drove closer to her, and Valerie saw her acquaintance get out of the car. He was clearly "on" something, and Valerie wondered if this explained why, instead of greeting her, he quickly walked away.

There was something else in the car, hidden from view — a machete.

On Sunday a news story of the vicious murder appeared in the morning edition of the local newspaper. Armand didn't see it, but Rita, who'd overheard the conversation between Valerie and Armand, and with whom Armand had discussed his anxious feelings, saw the article. Stunned, she called him.

"Armand, remember what you were saying Friday about Valerie?"

"Yes."

"Well, it happened."

"Oh, my God!" replied Armand. He listened to the article as Rita read it to him over the phone. Then, devastated, he hung up the receiver. If he had told Valerie **everything** he'd seen, would that have made a difference? Would she have listened to him and stayed home? It was a rhetorical question Armand could not answer. He thought briefly of calling the police with the information he'd perceived before the fact. He knew Jeff Cull at the Montaine Police Department for he'd worked recently with him on a murder case. It had been a matter of sheer coincidence at the time and was his first participation in detective/psychic teamwork. Still, Cull might be able to assure the Sommerville Police that he wasn't a crank.

"No," he decided. Even though Cull had been impressed with the details Armand had been able to give on the Patricia McCoy case, the Sommerville detectives were an unknown quantity.

"They won't believe me," he convinced himself. "They'll think I'm a crazy, because most cops don't believe in psychic things. I'd better sit tight."

The next morning, Monday, September 18, Armand opened the door of his Fontana office to begin a day of clairvoyant readings. Valerie's vicious murder was still uppermost in his mind. By now he had begun to realize that Valerie was such a strongminded person that she wouldn't have heeded his warnings even if he had shared the gory details of what he had perceived as her death.

"There's a time to come into life and a time to go out," Armand often philosophized. Although some deaths can be prevented if the person is warned and takes evasive action, Valerie's death could not have been prevented. His intuition told him that this had been a *karmic* situation.

Getting ready for his round of half-hour appointments, for which he charged each client a modest fee, Armand saw a small package lying on his desk. It seemed vaguely familiar. Picking it up, he realized it contained Valerie's business cards of which she'd been so proud.

Using the business cards as a psychometric object, Armand slipped into a light trance. Almost immediately he saw Valerie standing before him. He was a little startled at the ease with which the cards provided the bridge into the other dimension, for he had discovered long ago that metal holds more psychic vibrations than other materials and preferred to work with a client's ring or watch or other pieces of jewelry to draw out impressions. But here was Valerie, almost as solid as life. The spirit-form was wearing her favorite tight black pants which tied around the ankles and a gaily colored blouse with the ends gathered into a knot in front, showing off her slim waist. The prized business cards, on which she'd left her vibrations, had allowed the murdered woman's spirit to manifest before him.

"You were right, Armand," Valerie told him. "I should have listened to you. I was too strong-headed, and that's what got me killed. I was mad, too, and wanted to get away. I was afraid Carlos was going to follow after me and take me home. He'll be called in for questioning, but **he didn't do it!**"

"It was horrible, Armand," continued Valerie, sharing with him details of her gruesome death. "They did it while I was still conscious, you know, but it's all over now. Try to get the one who walked away from the car — the one I knew — to come forward. He can tell the police who the other two were."

After Valerie's spirit vanished back into the other dimension from which she had materialized, Armand went on with his life. But Valerie's murder continued to bother him, and he knew he had to do something about it. He read the scant articles which appeared in the local press; they stated that witnesses had seen Valerie getting into a car with two young men. Her husband, Carlos, was picked up for questioning but was released. Armand remained reluctant to contact the police on his own.

His reluctance was understandable but, in a way, unnecessary. Only a few months before, he'd had a successful contact with a Montaine, California detective on a case concerning another young murdered woman. Armand, in spite of his local fame as an outstanding clairvoyant, had never been approached by detectives seeking help on puzzling crimes. His involvement with the case of Patricia McCoy occurred unexpectedly and in a roundabout fashion, and the twist of fate by which the incident was woven into the fabric of his life seems to indicate that Armand was destined to become deeply enmeshed in psychic/detective work.

On a cold day late in December 1977 a young man came to Armand's Fontana office seeking a reading. He wished to consult Armand about certain career decisions, for he had heard that the clairvoyant was very talented in giving this kind of advice. The farthest thing from this young man's mind was murder or Armand's peculiar budding talent in crime detection.

During this reading, Armand perceived an aura near the young man (whose name to this day is unknown to us). It was not the young man's aura from which Armand was perceiving details of his life. **This** aura was that of a young woman whom the man had recently dated and who lived in the same apartment complex.

Curious as to why the woman's aura should display so prominent-
ly in the tiny office, Armand reached out with his mind into it.

"I was able to perceive her aura as well as his because he had dated
her very recently," Armand explained later. "They had gone together
to a party or a show. Her aura was still around him because their date
was one of the last things she would ever do in this life."

Finding the girl's time track within her aura, Armand saw her leaving a party with a stranger, getting into her sportscar with him and driving off. Then he saw the car parked in a lot near her apartment building
and — her body lying dead in an alleyway nearby.

He tried to warn the young man who was sitting in front of him
about what he had envisioned.

"There's a young lady close to you," Armand remembers saying.
"She either **was** murdered or is going to be murdered in two weeks, two
months, something like that. She lives in an apartment with another
girl, the same apartment house where **you** live, and you've dated her
recently. **Warn her about this!**" he emphasized. "Tell her she's got to
be careful around the holidays," he continued, for the information was
coming in clearer now. "Tell her she'll meet a stranger at a party and
leave with him. But I see her lying murdered in an alleyway, with one
shoe on and the other one lying nearby. The murderer is stabbing her
repeatedly."

The young man didn't know how to react to Armand's warning.
He'd come to get details about his **own** life. He dated several young
women and couldn't make any real sense out of what the clairvoyant
was saying.

Armand finished the reading on the young man's own time track
and thought no more about it. The client had recorded the interview,
and the clairvoyant assumed he would act on it.

Two weeks later Detective Jeff Cull of the Montaine Police Department telephoned him. He rather hesitantly described how a young man
had brought in a tape recording of one of Armand's sessions, requesting
that Cull listen to it. This young man had, a few days previously, been
called in for questioning on a murder case. A young woman, Patricia
McCoy, had been found dead of stab wounds in an alleyway adjacent
to her apartment building in Montaine. All her acquaintances had been
routinely interviewed.

The strange coincidence of Patricia's death jogged the young man's
memory. Questioned by the Montaine police about Patricia McCoy's
death, the puzzle fell together in his mind. He played the tape of
Armand's reading again; the description of Patricia and the facts of

her grisly death were accurate, and he **had** dated Patricia off and on. In fact, the last time they went out together was very close to the time of his session with the psychic.

He took the tape to Detective Cull, the Montaine PD officer who had questioned and then released him once it had become evident that he had had nothing to do with Patricia's death.

While speaking with Detective Cull on the phone, Armand offered to try to pick up added details on the case and suggested that Cull bring an object associated with Patricia McCoy to aid him in his reading. Metal objects like jewelry were best, explained Armand, or a piece of clothing the deceased was wearing at the time of death. If these were unavailable, any object associated with Miss McCoy would be helpful.

Detective Cull appeared at Armand's Fontana trailer shortly afterward carrying a picture of the dead girl. He was glad to learn that Armand would not charge for his services, for Cull was doing this without official approval and would be hard pressed to explain what a psychic's fee was doing on his expense account! Taking the picture Cull offered him, Armand perceived again the circumstances of the girl's murder. He described the details to Cull as they unfolded before him. The picture of the dead woman had sufficient vibrations of Patricia McCoy about it to allow Armand to slip his consciousness into the girl's time track which led up to the events of her death. However, Patricia's spirit did not appear to him as Valerie's would do months later. Patricia was completely unknown to him in the material world, and the picture lacked sufficient live vibrations to enable him to receive an adequate response.

Jeff Cull was impressed with Armand's reading, nevertheless. The case had run out of leads and he personally felt he had nothing to lose by accepting Armand's offer of help, especially in view of the information on the tape recording the victim's acquaintance had asked him to listen to. Cull returned to his station, determined to follow up on Armand's suggestion — that a lead to the murderer might be gotten from interviewing the participants of the party Patricia McCoy had attended the evening of her death. Hopefully, someone might remember who the "stranger" had been whom she had met that night and with whom she had left.

A few months later, Detective Cull was interviewed by a staff reporter for the prestigious *Los Angeles Times* (San Gabriel Valley Section). Çull spoke freely about his reaction to Armand's reading on the Patricia McCoy case.

"I was floored. It blew my mind," the detective was quoted.

"I showed him a picture of the victim and he described the crime scene in detail... I was very impressed with the guy."

"He enabled us to narrow down the investigation, and we confirmed through him how we thought the direction of the case should go."

"He knows so much, you think maybe he's the suspect, which is crazy." Cull was also quoted in another article in the San Gabriel Valley *Tribune*. He told reporter Linda Haugsted, *Tribune* staff writer, that the psychic had brought out "very unusual aspects" of the Patricia McCoy case. "An outsider would have only one chance in 10,000 of guessing the facts." At the time this article was written, Cull confirmed that the Montaine police were still investigating that murder.

Shortly after Valerie Montes' murder, Cathy Armstrong, a *Sun* writer, interviewed Armand about his clairvoyant practice. Word of the psychic's counseling skill was being spread by word of mouth. Armand was never one to advertise, but clients were nevertheless flooding to his Fontana trailer office; he was booking them a week in advance, seven to eight sessions each day. It was a situation the woman reporter couldn't resist.

This article in the *Sun* newspaper (based in San Bernardino, California) was basically a human interest piece, covering many facets of Armand's clairvoyant ability. Armand told of foreseeing the death of John Paul I.

"I told my friends," he was quoted. "The Pope won't live out the month, let alone the year. I saw it right there; it just came like a flash."

In that same vision, according to Armstrong's article, he saw the next Pope (John Paul II) assassinated in St. Peter's Square within three to five years. As we know now, this charismatic churchman survived nearly fatal wounds as a result of an assassination attempt, which occurred while he was greeting the faithful in a huge crowd in St. Peter's Square on May 13, 1981, two and one-half years after Armand's prediction. The five-year period Armand mentioned was completed toward the end of 1983. Admirers of this holy man can only be thankful that extra precautions have forestalled another assassin and that this prediction of untimely death was prevented from occurring.

In this same 1978 *Sun* article Armand also predicted that Christ would be reborn and reveal himself by the end of 1986. The churches would then be united and governed by a group of men rather than by one Pope. Armand is interested in reports from England that there is, at the present time, a holy man who preaches every Saturday in the Pakistani section of London. He does not claim to be Christ but calls himself the "Disciple of Light." Many articles have been written about him in various newspapers around the world. Three of Armand's clients have personally heard him speak. They told Armand that when the man walks into the large crowds who gather around him, a strange and peaceful "warmth" radiates out from him, encompassing all those present in its invisible glow.

For purposes of this present volume, however, the most important thing Armand spoke of to Cathy Armstrong was the murder of his former employee, Valerie Montes. She wrote his account of his warning to Valerie and her subsequent violent death.

"Somebody witnessed the thing (murder) and I want him to go and ask for police protection, because he's afraid," Armand was quoted. He also stated the witness was a young Latino man and that the murder was gang related. He predicted the killers would be eventually arrested.

To the best of Armand's knowledge, the murder of Valerie Montes has not been solved. The article in the paper, in which he pleaded for the young man to come forward, did not produce the results he wished for. The man has not yet come forward, probably because he fears for his own life. But the article set in motion a series of events which led to Armand's becoming deeply involved in detective/psychic teamwork and, eventually, to the writing of this book.

Cathy Armstrong's article was read by many in the Victor Valley area and beyond, and some open-minded police officers among the readership were alerted to the fact that an accomplished clairvoyant was available in the area. Like most parts of the United States, Southern California detectives hesitated to even consider (out loud) the practicability of consulting psychics on unsolved cases. However, as future events revealed, the idea was being nurtured in the minds of certain law enforcement officers.

Shortly after Armstrong's article appeared, a Sommerville, California detective called Armand. Detective Don Keaton had been assigned the case of Valerie Montes. It had been six full weeks since her death, and all leads had petered out. Independent witnesses had seen Valerie standing near the corner phone booth and had seen her being forced into a car by two young men, but these witnesses were unable to help the police locate the killers.

In his conversation with Detective Keaton, Armand told the officer what he had perceived about the murder, both before and after the fact. Keaton expressed amazement at the details known to the clairvoyant, especially non-published facts about the manner in which she had been butchered by her sadistic assailants. Armand suggested to Keaton that the police should try to establish contact with the third young man who could point the finger at the actual killers. Aside from this, however there was nothing concrete which Armand could suggest toward solving the crime. The police had waited too long; leads were gone and clues were cold. Most importantly, Valerie's spirit would not reappear again to Armand. The clairvoyant felt she was at peace and tranquil in the ethereal dimension and had no real reason for returning temporarily to offer help on the case.

This was not an uncommon situation in Armand's experience. Although he was to experience marked success in many future cases in contacting the spirit of murdered persons (including the other cases discussed in detail in this book), Valerie's murder had been, Armand felt, the result of a karmic debt. Once the debt was paid, her spirit was able to advance onto a higher level of spiritual existence, and she felt no need of returning to help solve the crime.

"This is why Valerie would rush everything," explained Armand in an interview for this book. She did things well and very thoroughly, but it was like she was rushing toward death. She couldn't **wait!** Everything had to be **fast.** "I'm also sure she subconsciously sensed that her death was near that last Friday morning. She said she had all these calls to make, and had called her mother to settle some personal problem between them. She was so **pleased** she had **done** it. She was doing things she had to get out of her system. Subconsciously she was trying to say hello and goodby to a lot of people."

"I feel in a past life she had murdered someone and in this life she had to be murdered to know what it was. What you do to others, you get back. That's the basis of karmic reality. So once she had fulfilled this, she was able to grow into a higher spiritual level."

Armand's perception of why Valerie died young was doubly disturbing to him. He had lost a valued friend and employee in Valerie, but there was another person close to him who was demonstrating a similar, rushing personality. His young friend, Raymond Lewellyn, whom Armand jokingly called "son" and who, in return, non-jokingly called Armand "Dad," was only twenty-one, but in Raymond's life there was never enough **time.** Everything he wanted had to happen — **fast!**

After Detective Keaton left his office, Armand thought again, uneasily, about Raymond and the anxiety which had begun to tap on the rim of the clairvoyant's consciousness. Would Raymond, like Valerie, also die young?

Armand again forced the anxiety down deep into his subconscious and began to wonder why Detectives Cull and Keaton hadn't contacted him to tell him what happened on the cases. He wondered in vain. Early in his new career, Armand had come up against the main block which hampers detective/psychic teamwork. He would continue to give his services and information freely to any law enforcement officer who might have the foresight and courage to request them, but Armand would receive almost no feedback in return.

Because of understaffing and underbudgeting of police departments, law officers have little time to give feedback on cases to those who help them with clues and leads. And there was yet another stronger reason why Detectives Cull and Keaton could not return to Armand on the McCoy and Montes cases. Any information given by Armand — or any other psychic — which might lead to a break in a case could not be regarded as "legally obtained evidence." For what court in the land would consider the word of a psychic as "probable cause?" These considerations aside, one can only wonder what advancements could be made in detective/psychic teamwork if the psychic was given confidential feedback as soon as possible. Feedback is helpful to all psychics, even the most talented, and for many it can be vital. One thing became clear in Armand's life. He made up his mind to devote all his time and energy as a professional clairvoyant. He could make a modest living by charging clients moderate fees — but his services would be free to any law enforcement officials who might seek his help. In this way, he could serve his fellow men.

CHAPTER TWO

"The Man Who Hated 'Pigs' "

The news of Armand's amazing accuracy spread rapidly, though furtively, through the Montaine and Sommerville Police Departments. Detectives Cull and Keaton were still receiving flak from skeptical fellow officers over their unorthodox source of information. In spite of the friendly ridicule, however, they realized logically that Marcotte had some kind of perceptive talent which could be used by police in helping to solve violent crimes. They couldn't explain what the talent **was**, or how he got a handle on it, but you don't argue with success.

Detectives in adjoining cities become acquainted with each other in the course of their work, and so word about the psychic in Fontana spread to Overton, a city of 30,350 population adjacent to Montaine. Overton's police force was composed of fifty-two full-time officers and twenty-five reserves, not including the dozen office workers who kept its files in proper order.

A generation ago, vineyards had covered much of Overton's wide expanse, but now a busy, modern city had sprung up — a balanced society of industry, retail commerce, service and professional persons. And like any modern American city, it had its full share of violent crime.

When Detective Robert Costas of the Overton Police Department heard about Cull's and Keaton's experiences, he decided to try an experiment. Out of his files he pulled an unsolved murder which, because of its particularly vicious nature, had continued to disturb him deeply.

He got Armand's telephone number from Jeff Cull, called Armand and briefly described how he'd been working on a double murder case for over a year and a half, but that the investigation had ground to a halt — there were no more clues to follow up. Would Marcotte consider giving him an appointment to see if he could be of assistance in the matter? An appointment was set for the following Tuesday, the day Armand reserved each week for working with police. Costas asked if he should bring anything relating to the crime with him.

"Bring as many objects as possible, like a wallet or belt buckle, or clothing the victims were wearing at the time of the murder," replied Armand. "Anything that hasn't been handled by a lot of other people. I prefer pieces of jewelry, however, because they seem to hold impressions better."

Costas showed up promptly on the appointed date, and the clairvoyant met him at the door of his unimposing office. As Costas placed his tape recorder on the small, crowded desk, Armand could feel his uneasiness, born of professional, but not unfriendly skepticism.

"I've brought you a ring and a watch the victims were wearing at the time they were killed," said Costas. "Now, what do you expect from me while you're doing this... uh, whatever it is you do?"

Armand laughed. He felt a good rapport with this big, ruddy-faced detective — an instantaneous feeling of comradeship. They would work well together, he was sure.

"The only other things that might help," he said, "are the victims' birthdates and the date and approximate time they died. However, these aren't necessary as long as I have the pieces of their jewelry to work from."

Eager to assist however he could, Costas called in to his department and received the requested information.

"You know," Armand ventured, "I feel we've worked together in a past life. Now we're going to work together again, but in different stations in this life." Costas seemed dumbfounded and made no reply; Armand perceived instantly the detective probably thought he was pretty weird. However, he sat down opposite the psychic at the small desk.

Armand picked up the watch. It was not running; it had been thought to have stopped at the time of the woman's death. "If I tell you the truth about what happened to these people," he commented, "this watch will start to run again."

Costas passed over this statement too; it seemed as if he wasn't sure how to respond. Instead, he asked Armand what he should do or say if he heard something in the reading that made sense to him.

"Well, if you hear something you know to be accurate at the crime scene, let me know by some little short sentence, so I'll know I'm on the right track. If I hit on something which seems crucial to you as a clue on how to further investigate the crime, say 'More detail, please,' and I will look deeper into that matter and my picture of that particular aspect will become clearer."

Costas nodded. No matter what he might be feeling inside — skeptical, puzzled, uncomfortable or maybe a little foolish — he managed to maintain a professional demeanor.

Armand chose to work with the male victim's ring first. He held it in his hand and cleared his mind of all personal problems and everyday responsibilities. He mentally counted backwards from 10 — 9, 8, 3, 0, and found himself in a familiar blankness, that twilight environment where no objects, not even "Armand," as himself, existed. He was just "there," a knowing consciousness seeking a certain place back in time. He rubbed the ring, thinking back to its owner on April 17, 1979, in the late evening.

He found himself in a small living room somewhere and perceived an olive-complexioned, middle-aged man with hazel eyes. He was staring intently in Armand's direction and scowling.

"I know what you want to do," he telepathed to Armand. "But I don't work with pigs! I hate their guts!"

Armand laughed softly and conveyed this bit of information to Costas. The detective chuckled and shifted his feet. He knew the male victim had been a former felon and had served time in the state penitentiary. However, he didn't share this with the psychic. It was only **after** this session that Armand would find out just why this hazel-eyed spirit hated "pigs."

He allowed the uncooperative spirit-form to fade into the blankness, then took up the woman's watch. Concentrating on its now-dead owner, he saw a figure of a nice-looking woman in her middle years appear in his inner sight. She was dark complexioned, with brown eyes and seemingly of Latin descent. Armand knew that **she** would help, for he felt an anxiety from her that the murders should be solved.

"The situation has gone on too long," she told him mentally. "It's been a big source of grief to my children, and I want the murderer caught."

With the link established, Armand's twilight vision began to clear. He was still in the small living room. Chairs and a couch came into view, then an undersized chandelier or hanging lamp gave additional light to the scene. A large round clock on the wall read 9:30. The building seemed to serve not only as living quarters but as some kind of office as well. He smelled paint and saw that renovations were going on.

He saw a man and woman in the place and recognized them as the two entities associated with the ring and the watch. They were talking together agreeably. The couple were married but had been separated for some time. Armand knew that the woman was moving in again with her husband, for they had recently managed to work out their difficulties together.

Armand perceived a car in a driveway outside the living room. "A man is getting out of a car that just pulled up," he told Costas. He was speaking in the present tense, for in his mind the events were unfolding before him. He had gone back in time more than a year — time travel which was considered a normal event in the process of "psi," or "remote-viewing," as scientists who have investigated this mysterious faculty have termed it.[1]

Armand then saw the two men talking in the small living room. The phone rang in the office section of the building, toward the back of the living quarters. The woman went to answer it, leaving the two men alone.

The two men finished speaking. They had evidently struck some kind of bargain, for they shook hands. What the conversation was about escaped Armand's perception. The man he had perceived first — the one who "hated pigs" — led his visitor down a small hall, past a kitchenette, a bathroom, a small bedroom alcove and into the office. He opened the back door and showed the man an L-shaped construction composed of many rooms, each with a number on the door.

Armand, meanwhile, was relating to Costas the events that were unfolding like visions in his mind. He assumed that the hazel-eyed man, who would be later identified as Joseph Casaneda, was the manager of a hotel or apartment building. He was puzzled, however, because there was no light in the passageway leading to the multiple doors.

"It's awfully dark in that hall," he commented to Costas. "They don't have any lights."

Costas nodded, indicating that Armand's description of the surroundings was helpful. Armand, encouraged, watched while Casaneda pointed out doors #7 and #11 to his visitor. He watched the other man depart.

"What happened then?" queried Costas.

"The woman's awfully tired. She's finished with the phone call and goes to lie down. She goes to sleep in the little bedroom alcove. The man sits in the living room. He's eating some fruit. There seems to be an apple and an orange there."

"OK," agreed Costas. "What happens next?"

Evidently a lapse of time had occurred in Armand's mind. "It's between 11:00 and 11:30 now," replied the clairvoyant. "Here comes that second man again. He's got a girl, a young woman, with him."

The woman seemed to be between twenty-three and twenty-nine years of age and was very attractive in a brash sort of way. Her skin was lighter than her companion's but still bespoke of partial Latin heritage. Armand relayed this information to Costas.

"They're talking about girls, the two men are," Armand continued. "The girl's standing there while the two men talk about **two** girls that were supposed to come. The girl says, 'Don't worry. I can do the work for both.' The other man assures the manager that she's capable, that she's 'prime,' that she can handle it."

Armand couldn't perceive what made her "prime." There is a particular lack of vulgarity in the World Mind, from which he was drawing his impressions. Because of the surroundings and the actions he perceived, the psychic assumed the girl might be there to clean rooms #7 and #11!

"The two men agree on using the one girl," continued Armand. "The other man leaves again after pointing out rooms #7 and #11. She starts off down the dark hall."

Following the young woman down the darkened passageway, he saw her knock on #7. A man and woman answered the door together. They didn't seem to be married to each other. The psychic saw through the open door that a TV was blaring in the room. The girl went into the room and closed the door.

Time passed again almost instantly in Armand's mind. He had related to Costas what he had seen, but did not follow the young woman into the room. After all, he hadn't been **asked** by the detective to do this. Since Costas had already stated his purpose — to get information about the murders of the Casanedas — **Armand was zeroing in only on that aspect.** Whatever was happening in room #7 evidently had nothing directly to do with the double killing.

"Did she go into any other room?" inquired the policeman. Armand's mind jumped instantly over a space of one and one-half hours. The next thing he saw was the attractive young woman coming out of #7 and proceeding to room #11. Two young men responded to her knock and welcomed her in. They were dressed in something like khaki, but Armand couldn't determine whether they were soldiers — or police! Another two hours passed briefly and then he saw the girl emerge from room #11. It was now about 2:30 in the morning.

The girl rejoined Casaneda in the small living room. He offered her a piece of fruit, then paid her some money. "I want **twice** this!" she declared hotly. "I did the work of two, and I want to be paid for two!"

Armand felt deepening concern. "Oh, they're arguing!" he declared to Costas. "She's saying, 'I want twice the price because I did the work for two,' and he's saying 'No.' "

Armand still did not perceive what kind of work she'd done. But he was to find out, very soon, in a most incredible way — from one of the murder victims himself.

Costas, meantime, seemed fascinated. The clairvoyant, in his reading, had hit upon numerous points of truth, including the fact that two pieces of half-eaten fruit had been found at the murder scene. The few apparent inaccuracies were possible misinterpretations.

Detective Costas had researched the tenants in both rooms which Armand had mentioned. In #7 a married man and his girl friend had spent the night and had hired a prostitute to participate in a sexual orgy. In room #11, two Marines had taken up lodging on April 17 and had used the same hooker to liven up the night. The "hotel" which Armand perceived was actually an X-rated, adults-only motel; the television which the psychic saw in room #7 had been spewing forth a pornographic film. And the open passageway which Armand had described as "a hallway without any lights" was actually an open space which led from room to room around the L-shaped motel complex. It was no wonder the psychic had not seen any lights, for the sky was clouded over; no stars or moon were visible in the darkened night.

Costas listened intently as Armand continued.

"This woman is giving him an awful lot of lip. They're sitting in the living room where the lamp hangs down from the ceiling. The girl is bitchy as anything. Now here comes the man to pick up the girl. He parks his car in the driveway, walks through the front door, and the girl tells him the manager won't pay her extra. He's mad as hell at the manager."

Armand heard the argument but could not make out all the details of the conversation. He got the impression that the other man wouldn't get his "share" if Casaneda didn't cough up more money. He saw the dark-skinned man pull a small handgun from his pocket and point it threateningly at the manager.

Armand felt panic. "Oh, my God! He was shot!" he exclaimed automatically, even though he heard no gunshot. What he perceived with forceful clarity, though, was the fear from the hazel-eyed manager, for the other man seemed to be high on drugs and was behaving irrationally.

The manager didn't want any more trouble.

"OK!" he agreed. "I'll give you more! I'll give you half what another girl would have made. But you didn't live up to **your** contract, you know. You promised two, and you only brought one!"

Casaneda turned his back on the furious pair and started toward the hall leading to the tiny office. Armand heard him mumbling and grumbling as he walked through the darkened kitchen. The manager didn't see the young woman pull something out of her purse, unfold it, and hand it to her angry companion, nor did he hear her whisper, "Use this!"

But Armand, perceiving the action back in time, saw it. "Wait a minute," he said to Costas. "He wasn't shot!" He described seeing the young woman pull a long, dark-handled knife from her purse, silently unfolding the sharp, gleaming blade. The dark man took it, realizing even through his drug-clouded mind that a knife could kill silently, while a gunshot would wake up the whole area. He was fuming; he scarcely realized what he was about to do.

"Wait a minute!" Armand raised his voice as he continued to describe the turn of events to Costas. "He wasn't shot!"

He was living in two different dimensions, talking to the detective, while watching the bizarre scene in visionary form before him.

"This is the last time you're gonna pull this shit on me," growled the girl's companion. "You're not gonna cheat me out of my share!"

Then Armand felt the thrusts of the knife as Casaneda was stabbed over and over again. Casaneda gave a loud moan and fell against the wall of the small kitchen. He collapsed and crumpled to the floor, dying almost instantly.

Armand tried to throw off most of the pain without losing the visual scene. Then he heard Casaneda's wife shout, "What's going on!" He saw her emerge from the bedroom alcove, clutching something around her neck.

"As she comes out, the man stabs her, too!" he informed Costas. "Five, ten times, seven for sure. Oh, God, she's bleeding!"

Costas listened intently, for the psychic had accurately described the position in which the two victims had fallen, the manner of death, and even perceived the fact that Alice Casaneda was clutching something around her — a blanket she had been sleeping in, wrapped around her like a cloak. The shock of the slashing blows had frozen the muscles of her hand; she continued to clutch the blanket protectively around her as she fell against the bathroom wall, knocking over a shelf which held several items, as well as an ironing board on which she had been pressing garments a few short hours before. She collapsed against this wall, apparently dead.

Then the killer turned back to Casaneda. In his mindless, brutal rage, he stabbed the victim repeatedly, making doubly sure he was dead. When he finally finished venting his fury, the manager's body bore between 20 and 30 stab wounds.

He returned to Mrs. Casaneda and made sure that she, also, would not live to identify the killers. Again and again the knife sliced through the blanket into her body, until the killer's anger was satisfied.

Armand followed the two assailants as they swiftly searched the little office, describing what he saw to Costas. He heard the murderer mutter, "I know it's here, **someplace!**" They threw open a metal box in which the hotel receipts and cash payments were kept, but ignored the money there. They were looking for something more valuable — something that could incriminate **them** if it ever fell into the hands of authorities. Finally they found an envelope, rifled swiftly through it and threw away some of the contents. They took some documents and something else Armand could not see and dashed out the back door.

Armand watched them hastily climb into the car which was parked headed toward the street. They roared it into life, screeched into a left turn and swiftly sped out of sight. The geraniums and ivy growing on the border of the driveway bent with the wind of their passage; then, everything was still.

"Go on," Costas urged.

The brief phrase directed Armand's attention back inside the living room. "Oh, my God!" he exclaimed. "The woman's not dead! She's getting up! She's hanging on to the wall. It's been newly painted white, but she's bleeding so bad the blood's running down her arms and hands. She's clutching at the wall and I see all the bloodstains on the wall. She's trying to get to a little stand, kind of a dresser with drawers that's in the office, where there's a phone. She's going to try to call for help!"

Armand, half feeling the woman's anguish, also was seeing as through her eyes. He realized that Alice Casaneda had probably lost consciousness for about ten minutes. Then, as her circulatory system temporarily revived, she had become aware of what had taken place. The heavy blanket she had clutched around her had helped deflect some of the knife wounds. They were not quite as deep as those which had killed her husband. Nevertheless, they were to be fatal, but not quite yet.

As the blood slowly drained from Alice Casaneda's body, her eyesight dimmed. Armand saw as **she** saw — a darkened hallway, past the bath, past the bedroom alcove in which she had taken her last sleep, toward the glow of a lamp which stood on the dresser beside the phone.

Frantically, Alice Casaneda made her way along the hall, the glow of the lamp fading as she inched along. As she grabbed the phone and sat on the couch in the tiny office, her sight failed entirely. She could not see to dial the numbers! She fell from the couch and lay on the floor. As she died, the receiver, off the hook, gave forth a useless dial tone.

Costas was sitting forward in his chair, remembering the grisly trail of bloody handprints along the newly painted wall of the small living quarters. In the course of the investigation, eighteen months before, he and his partner had surmised that the woman had tried to reach the phone to call for help; a trail of bloodstains from the bathroom wall to the phone had been mute evidence of this. Yet here was a psychic, who had never seen the murder locale, who had no logical knowledge of the details of the murders, describing the woman's death as if it were happening before his eyes. In a very real sense, it **was**.

"As she dies, she keeps saying, 'That damn Romano, that damn Romano!' " Armand told Costas. "That must be the name of the guy who killed these people."

Before Costas could answer, the psychic's mind was filled with a waterfall of facts. "She wants you to catch this 'Romano,' " he continued. "You've questioned this man before. He lied to you. He told you something that was a lie. He said he hadn't seen the murdered man for a long time, but you can check it out with the victims' son, and he'll confirm that Romano lied to you!"

The session seemed over, at least the vivid, visual part — the time trip back to the murder scene. Armand looked at the woman's watch in his hand, then listened to it. It was ticking. He handed it to Costas.

"Well, the watch is running," Armand said. "I told you it would if I told you the truth."

Costas took the watch, puzzled. Later, when interviewed by Linda Haugsted, *Tribune* staff writer, for a news article about the case, Costas was quoted, "My partner suggested I take the watch to a jeweler to see what's wrong with it, but I'm not sure I want to know."

The detective **did** want to know if he could verify the psychic's statements about the killing. There **was** a "Romano" he'd questioned early in the investigation — a felon who'd been a cellmate of Casanedas when the two were confined for a time in the state penitentiary. Romano had insisted he hadn't seen Casaneda since they were in prison together, and he had an alibi. He'd spent all that night with a young Latino woman, in her twenties, who had confirmed his statement. Her description sounded suspiciously like that of the "prime" girl whom Armand had envisioned at the murder locale.

During the initial lengthy investigation, since there were no obvious clues on the scene pointing to the identity of the killer or killers, the police had interviewed all the friends and relatives of the Casanedas. Even their children had been interviewed. Costas left the trailer, eager to start back on the cold trail by rechecking his files and talking with Casadena's son.

Shortly after the detective had returned to his office, Armand called him to recount some additional information..

"Detective Costas took the ring and watch which had belonged to the witnesses," Armand stated in an interview for this book. "But after the detective left, I kept thinking about the man victim, the one with the hazel eyes who'd said he wouldn't work with pigs. He came over in his spirit-form about ten minutes after Detective Costas left and he told me who his killer was. He said 'It was Romano who did it,' which was the same information I'd gotten through working with his wife's watch. He told me that Romano was a pimp and a drug pusher and that the young woman was a prostitute. He and Romano had been doing business together for some time. Romano would bring whores to the motel to service the guests.

"He wanted Romano caught, but he wouldn't tell me any of this while Detective Costas was in my office trailer. In fact," Armand said with a little sigh, "Romano didn't even accept the fact he was dead! And he still 'hated pigs'!"

After Casaneda's spirit-form was gone, Armand immediately phoned Costas, telling him about the surprising visit. Costas didn't seem to accept **all** that Armand told him, but he admitted to Armand that the facts of Casaneda's and Romano's histories were accurate.

Something which Armand had said about Casaneda puzzled Costas. The psychic had described the murdered man as having hazel eyes, and Costas was sure Casaneda had had brown eyes.

He questioned Armand about this, thinking an error had been made. Armand contended that Joe Casaneda's eyes were **hazel**, and advised the detective to check on it. The detective went back to the autopsy report to prove his **own** point. There, on the official record, he read: "Eyes Hazel."

Costas interviewed Casaneda's son, who stated he knew Romano by sight. He confirmed that he'd seen his father with Romano at least twice before the murders. One time was two weeks prior, and the second time just a few days before his parents met their deaths. Costas proceeded to pick up Romano.

He had no charges against him as far as the Casaneda murders were concerned, since even an accurate reading by a psychic cannot count as "probable cause" for arrest. However, Costas had also talked with one of Casaneda's daughters who, although she didn't know Romano personally, had heard about him from her father.

Romano was put in a lineup which Casaneda's daughter attended. When she viewed Romano through the one-way mirror, she felt a sense of hatred and terrible cold, even though she'd never seen the man before. She pointed him out to the police, confiding that she had the feeling her dead parents were trying to help her identify their killers.

This identification, eerie and puzzling even to the hardened investigators, still did not amount to legal evidence of any guilt. The police had to let Romano go free.

Searching for a reason to rearrest him, Costas found some outstanding traffic warrants against Romano. He was picked up again; this time he was held for five days. During that period he was requestioned about his whereabouts on April 17, 1979, without specifically being charged with the crime. Romano was extremely nervous during the interrogation but reiterated his former alibi — the dark-haired prostitute.

Meanwhile, the girl, frightened over the turn of events, fled the city. Costas was unable to learn her whereabouts, although Armand felt she was somewhere in Mexico or Texas.

Without the girl to question, and having no legal evidence that Romano's alibi for the evening of April 17, 1979 was phony, the police had to release him again after a friend made bail for him on the traffic charges. Taking advantage of his good luck, Romano wasted no time. He immediately skipped bail and fled; probably, as Armand comments ironically, he rejoined his dark-haired "prime" companion.

Privately, Costas was convinced that Romano was the Casanedas' murderer. His reinvestigation of the case, based on what Armand had been able to tell him, and the blunt proof that the man had lied about not having seen Casaneda for many months before the murders, constituted proof in his mind. But it was not enough to convince the courts.

Costas, unlike other detectives who secretly use psychics on difficult cases, had the courage to speak out publicly on the case. In a *Los Angeles Times* article, he expressed his mixture of satisfaction and puzzlement.

"If I didn't know better, I'd have arrested him (the psychic) for the double murders because there were too many things he told me he couldn't have known," he commented to the *Times* reporter. "I had my doubts, but during our first conversation the clairvoyant said I had important information in my files that I had forgotten about. A check of my files showed he was right.

"The information concerned a person I had interviewed in connection with the crime," Costas' quote continued. "The clairvoyant said this person was important in the investigation so I double-checked and found the person had lied when I first interviewed him."

In another article in the San Gabriel Valley Daily *Tribune*, which also concerned the Casaneda case, staff writer Linda Haugsted quoted Detective Costas, "He, (the psychic) mentioned a name and told me to go back and check. He said...the person lied. He helped me to get back on the right track."

The *Tribune* article specified that Costas had contacted the clairvoyant "as an experiment," following a recommendation by (now) Sergeant Jeff Cull of the Montaine Police Department. Haugsted's piece further confirmed other facts of the detective/psychic teamwork as set forth in this chapter.

Armand's knowledge of the murders on which he works invariably stops at a certain point. He is sometimes kept informed of a few ongoing events by grateful police, but usually they do not have time or opportunity to keep in close touch with him. However, in the Casaneda case he did receive some feedback about the arrest of Romano, the interrogation of the suspect, and Romano's extreme nervousness. Without this feedback, the facts of the Casaneda case would be lost in the limbo of secrecy which necessarily surrounds most of Armand's detective/psychic work.

Perhaps, in the larger scheme of things, this feedback was meant to happen. Without sample cases such as this, about which Armand feels free to talk, this book could not be written. Only by full explanation of sample cases can the mysterious and complicated process of detective/psychic cooperation be fully understood. We hope, as public understanding grows, that this process will be used openly by police departments throughout the country without fear of ridicule or reprisal.

CHAPTER THREE

"The Disappearance of Lucy Brady"

Lucy Brady was missing, and her son Stan was worried. It was not like his 77-year-old mother to go off alone without telling someone where she was. Stan had tried to contact her several times, but none of her neighbors in the trailer park had seen her for days. Lucy had no really close friends. She lived alone, kept mostly to herself and in general was dispirited and discontent.

Her car was gone from her carport, and her mobile home seemed, from the outside, deserted. Stan unlocked the door of the large mobile complex and looked around inside. What he saw convinced him that something must be very wrong. Not that the rooms weren't neat, well-vacuumed, and with every piece of furniture in place. The large glass sliding door, through which his mother habitually liked to look out at her small world, was sparkling clean as usual. But in the small kitchen sink there were unwashed dishes and on her bed, dresses, lingerie and stockings were scattered about. Since some of her best clothes were missing, and her luggage gone, Stan surmised that his mother had hastily packed for an unannounced trip.

Stan, however, knew that his mother was a finicky, meticulous housekeeper and **never** left dishes unwashed or clothes scattered about. She invariably left her trailer in apple-pie order when leaving to shop for small items or to share a social meal at the local seniors' activity center.

With increasing anxiety, Stan Brady talked over the situation with his brother in Texas and all their other relatives around the country. No one had heard from Lucy. Her son in Texas had expected her for

Thanksgiving, but it was now November 10, 1979, and he hadn't yet heard from her about final preparations for this trip.

Stan informed the local police about his missing mother. The Overton police investigation yielded a few more facts. A check at the nearby Senior Nutrition Activity Program (SNAP) revealed that she had lunched there on October 17 but had not been seen since. Neither had she confided in anyone there her plans for leaving town.

Slowly, other bits of puzzling information surfaced. In Lucy Brady's end-of-the-month mail there was a bill for a Visa card purchase of gasoline. It was from a La Habra, California gas station for the amount of $16.50. The license plate number on the bill was that of Lucy's green Nova, and Stan confirmed that the signature on the receipt seemed to be his mother's. Stan also learned that she had withdrawn $1,500 from her savings account a day or two before her disappearance.

These slim pieces of evidence indicated that Lucy Brady was probably alive and well, but she was simply not the type of person to take off without informing members of her family. Yet the material evidence pointed to the fact she had planned a trip, had packed and departed hastily and had taken a southeasterly route, since La Habra is twenty miles southeast of Overton.

Despite normal police procedures, the official investigation ground to a halt for lack of clues. But Stan Brady was the kind of man who fought his own battles. He chanced to read about a psychic group who worked with detectives in the Los Angeles Basin area. The group was called PsiCom. Stan lost no time. By mid-November he had made contact with the group and met personally with them on November 26, 1979, at the home of PsiCom's director, Dr. Louise Ludwig. He brought a thimble which belonged to his mother, for the group needed an object closely associated with the missing person for purpose of psychometry.

At their request, Stan told them nothing about his mother except that she had been missing for over a month. Working in turn with the thimble, each of the five members of the team silently wrote down their impressions concerning Lucy Brady's disappearance on PsiCom report forms. There was absolutely no exchange of information or conversation between them.

The team — composed at that time of four women and one man — came up with many correlating impressions which matched Lucy Brady's actual appearance, personality, emotional state and personal habits. The consensus was that she was small in stature, thin, with short graying hair. They described her as having hazel eyes and married twice, with two children. They also perceived that she had worked in sales before her retirement, that she was a worrier, unsure of herself, unhappy with her life, and had poor health.

Stan Brady confirmed that all these perceptions were correct. But he had no way of knowing whether the psychics' impressions of what had happened to her were just as correct. All five agreed that she was in an unhappy, perhaps confused state of mind and had decided to take a trip to get away from her problems. Two saw her in a hospital setting, perhaps amnesic or otherwise unable to call relatives for help. They could not agree on where she was, but two suggested the San Francisco area. Two others suggested that she had traveled in an easterly direction through Needles and Brawley, or even as far as the southeastern section of Colorado.

All of the psychics perceived that she was living, though perhaps ill and in a hospital setting, and the consensus was that eventually she would return home.

Besides the correct consensual information, individual members of PsiCom came up with correct information about Lucy Brady's personal habits — that she often hummed to herself, liked to look out a large window in her home, and often wore a favorite pink-and-white shawl.

Stan was impressed with PsiCom's abilities. Although they had given no definite leads on where to find his mother, he took the information back to the Overton police. Sergeant Edward Thomas of that department had been assigned to the case.

Meanwhile, word of Armand Marcotte's work with local law enforcement agencies had become general knowledge among police officers in various cities and towns surrounding Victor Valley. When Stan Brady brought the news of PsiCom's correct perceptions of his mother's appearance and personality, Sergeant Thomas made a hard decision. His colleague, Detective Costas, had been urging him to try working with Armand on an unsolved case so that he could prove to himself that psychically derived data could sometimes be very helpful.

Sergeant Thomas decided he wanted to try. The Lucy Brady case was the sort of case in which police were slowly beginning to seek psychic input — **a missing person where foul play was suspected but where all clues had led to dead ends.** Sergeant Thomas knew that Armand worked confidentially and without pay. Above all, he sought no publicity or credit for his work.

Sergeant Thomas called Armand to set up an appointment. He was prepared to launch into a discussion about the missing woman he was trying to find, but Armand cut him short.

"I don't want to know any details," the psychic said, as he checked his calendar book for an open time. "I'm glad to try to help, but all I want and need is the victim's birth date and date of disappearance."

"OK," replied Thomas, rather puzzled. "Is that all?"

"Since this is a missing person and not a confirmed murder victim." he was told, "bring me something from the home or where they were last seen living — something they might have been particularly fond of."

Thomas went to Lucy Brady's home. He chose a jewelry box from her dressing table, figuring logically that a woman going on a trip might rummage through her jewelry, trying to decide which items to take along. The detective arrived at Armand's office at the appointed time, carrying the jewelry box. Agreeing to the psychic's suggestion that he be told nothing about the disappearance, Thomas sat down beside the disordered desk. He supplied Armand with the woman's birth date and date of disappearance. He gazed around the cramped office as the clairvoyant opened the box and began to handle the pieces of jewelry one by one.

They were, for the most part, costume jewelry which every woman collects to wear with various dresses and suits. As he picked up a particular pair of pink earrings, Armand began to receive strong impressions.

"The information came in very strong," he explained later. "I started telling the detective that the lady lived in a mobile home, a very attractive place, in sort of a senior citizen environment. I kept getting that she lived alone and had a lot of money, but kept her good jewelry in a metal box in her home, and that this metal box also contained a lot of cash.

"I also kept getting that she'd been married twice and that she had divorced her second husband, and that there were some problems with him at the time of her disappearance."

Paradoxically, Armand kept receiving **positive** vibrations from the pink earrings. He felt that Lucy Brady was happy-go-lucky and excited as she packed for her trip. She had left these vibrations on the pink earrings as she had fondled them, trying to decide whether to take them with her. She had decided against it, according to Armand's impressions, and dropped them back into the box, where her emotional vibrations lay dormant until reactivated by the psychic's hands.

"I learned later," explains Armand, "that her son, and of course the police, had thought she was depressed and despondent at the time of her disappearance. "Yet I remember those earrings. They were pink and very attractive-looking. I could see a woman in her late sixties or early seventies, very active and very happy. She was intending to visit her sister. I kept getting her going toward Texas, or at least toward Highway 91 going south. Then I got that she was going to meet her boyfriend and take off and get married."

In the first session with Sergeant Thomas, Armand had no idea whether the information he was giving to the policeman was **known to the officer or not.** He wasn't getting any feedback from him, so he suggested to Thomas that if he was saying anything that might be helpful in the investigation, Thomas could indicate this by saying "More information" or some little phrase like it. He saw a gleam of interest in the detective's eyes when he mentioned Lucy Brady's reason for going on a trip. The detective indicated he wanted to hear more.

"I keep getting that she was going to meet her boyfriend and take off and get married," continued Armand. "He'd told her not to tell **anyone,** that they'd just run off and get married. They'd take a honeymoon trip to her sister who lived in Texas and surprise her by just turning up."

Thomas remembered that one of PsiCom's psychics had written on her report form, "Her sister is very important to her." He motioned to Armand to continue on that same idea.

"I keep getting the man wearing a khaki uniform, like a policeman, maybe," continued the clairvoyant. "He's five to eight years younger than this woman, but she looks young for her age. She knows him very well. **I think she's even been married to him before,** and this will be the second time around for them."

"But **he** didn't come and get her, you see," explained Armand to Thomas. "He's hired two young people, a young couple, to come to her house to tell her **he** couldn't meet her, but to go with this young couple and they'll take her to him. These young people come to the house, and the woman doesn't suspect anything. She packs real hurriedly, even left dishes in the sink, which she never does, because she's a very neat housekeeper. But she's **happy** about going, so she went. They all leave together in her light-colored car, a late model."

Thomas thought of Lucy Brady's '79 Nova. How did Armand know she even owned a car? And why was this psychic describing Lucy as happy, when all five PsiCom psychics perceived her as despondent and dissatisfied with her life, a fact confirmed by the missing woman's son?

He sat still and listened as Armand continued his twenty-five-minute reading. Thomas was taping the interview; he could ask Detective Costas to help him sort it out later.

"It takes awhile for the young people to guide the woman to the man who wears the khaki uniform. She's confused at one point and argues they must be going the wrong way," continued Armand.

Then the psychic seemed to sense something wrong. "Oh!" he exclaimed. "In the meantime, the man she's planning on marrying — the guy who's been her husband once before — sneaks into her home and rips her off. He takes this metal box of hers, with the money and the jewelry. I feel she's withdrawn something like $1,500 from the bank just a short time before to help pay expenses on their honeymoon. She never realizes he stole the things in the metal box."

The psychic's forehead crinkled in concern. "She's made two other withdrawals recently, also, both for $1,500, and both of those, too, in connection with this."

"Well," he continued, "they get to the place where she meets this man, and the young people get out of the car. They start on their trip to her sister's. She's so happy, and she'd kept her word to this man not to tell anyone about their plans, not even her sons or her sister. She's very much in love with this man."

With the detective listening intently, Armand described how the pair took off, heading toward Texas. The young people didn't figure in it anymore. They'd been innocent victims, hired by this man to bring her to a meeting-place. They'd had no idea he was stealing her possessions while they purposely, on his instructions, had wasted a little time guiding her in the wrong direction.

The pink earrings kept feeding information to him. He saw them buying gas for the car and the woman signing for it on a credit card. Then he saw the man take the wheel, and they drove on past Indio, or somewhere in that area.

Somewhere in the desert — Armand could not perceive just where — he felt that the man had either beaten the woman and forced her out of the car, or left her wandering around in the desert in a drugged state. He felt that the man then abandoned the car somewhere and took a bus back to his own home.

Sergeant Ed Thomas, in his logical mind, knew that **part** of the information Armand Marcotte had given him was accurate and verified, such as the description of the woman's home, her hasty departure, her three bank withdrawals of $1,500 each, the fact she'd stopped for gas and paid for it on her credit card. There was no rational way this mild-mannered psychic could know these things, unless Stan Brady had told him. But **that** didn't make sense either, for Brady did not know whom

Thomas had chosen as a second psychic source. He remembered hearing Detective Cull's excited words, "(Marcotte) knows so much, you'd think **he** was the suspect, but that's crazy!"

Thomas took the tape recording back to the police station and played it for Detective Costas. Costas, too, was impressed by the accuracies. They invited Stan Brady to hear the tape, hoping that he could tell whether or not the other statements made by Armand made any sense.

Stan Brady was more than impressed. Hearing Armand's taped description of Lucy's happiness over a pending remarriage, he could confirm one fact: his mother had been married to, and divorced from, a man several years her junior, who was a uniformed security guard at her mobile home complex!

For the first time Stan began to feel hopeful. Marcotte had not determined his mother was dead, and neither had any of the members of PsiCom. Perhaps there was hope that she would be found alive.

He could not explain why the PsiCom members, working from his mother's thimble, had perceived her as despondent and lonely, while Armand Marcotte, working with a pair of pink earrings, had seen her as excited and happy over a secret remarriage.

The police, however, now had a new lead — the security guard who had once been married to Lucy Brady. They brought him in for questioning. They could not accuse him of the crime on the strength of the psychic's statements, for this method of obtaining information would not hold up in the courts under the legal definition of "probable cause." The man seemed willing to talk with them and maintained stoutly throughout the lengthy interview that he knew nothing about Lucy Brady's disappearance. Unable to break down his story, the police were forced to let him go.

"In the meantime," explained Armand during the writing of this book, "I'd meditate on the case, trying to get added information to help the police. I began to get vivid, recurrent impressions that the woman was dead. I kept getting that the man had actually killed her and buried her next to an old shed somewhere in the desert. I could see the shed plainly; it was isolated and uncared for. The paint was peeling off; it was somewhere in the desert between San Bernardino, and Albuquerque. I know that's an awful big area, but I couldn't place it. It bothered me, because I could see her lying there, buried real shallowly, and one of her legs was sticking partway out of the dirt."

"About this time, the police came back to me on the case and asked me to do some more work. I told them I thought the woman was dead, and I guess they took me at my word because things really began to happen."

What happened was a rare and fortuitous event — not fortunate for Lucy Brady, but for the cause of detective/psychic teamwork. The story of Thomas's sessions with Armand came to the attention of a staff writer on the *Los Angeles Times*. The writer on this influential newspaper interviewed Sergeant Thomas, who gave permission for certain of his statements to be printed. And without such publicity, this case could not have been used for this book.

The reason for this lies in the fact that the work done by Armand for various police and sheriff departments, as well as other law enforcement agencies, is on a basis of strict confidentiality, as will be explained in Chapter Four. For reasons of their own, however, the four detectives (and their cases we have discussed so far) have received publicity in the press, including the fact that help was sought from a psychic (Marcotte) in the hope that new clues or leads could be obtained through this unconventional method. Therefore, Armand feels free to talk about these four sample cases, provided the names and locations are changed to protect the victim's families.

In the *Times* article, Sergeant Thomas was quoted as saying, "...we had run out of leads so I turned to the clairvoyant. Using only the date of her birth and an article of her jewelry, but no picture, he was able to give an accurate description of her. That kind of won my confidence.

"He indicated someone she knew had something to do with her disappearance and that that person had introduced her to two younger people who met her at her trailer to arrange to take her someplace."

Thomas was not reluctant to talk to the *Times* reporter about the search for Lucy Brady because he had no **material evidence** that a crime had been committed. But he understandably sidestepped giving precise details on the case, in the event an arrest could be made later. He expressed his personal opinion in the *Times* article that she was not missing by choice. He described how all her relatives had been contacted and how he had finally made the decision to contact "Mr. X" (as Armand was referred to in the article) after Lucy Brady's apparent signature turned up in La Habra on the Visa charge.

Acting on Armand's later impressions that the woman was dead and buried in a shallow grave in the desert near a wooden shed, Thomas described his subsequent actions.

"I put teletypes out," Thomas was quoted, "and contacted all the coroners' offices from San Bernardino to Arizona and New Mexico. Members of the Inyo County Sheriff's Office flew over the desert looking for her.

"None of this proves that she is deceased or the victim of foul play," Thomas continued, displaying the typical caution of the professional policeman. "But her disappearance just doesn't fit her character."

Convinced by the possible efficacy of detective/psychic teamwork, Sergeant Thomas accepted the aid of another clairvoyant who offered his help on the Brady case. This clairvoyant, who also remained anonymous, gathered impressions about the missing woman by concentrating on items of her clothing and a picture of her. He then spent Christmas Day 1979 exploring a section of San Bernardino County where he felt the woman was buried.

"I'm turning nobody away [who offers help] on this," Thomas was quoted in the *Times* article. "I'm getting frustrated but I haven't given up."

Here was a law enforcement officer who had the courage of his convictions. In spite of friendly ribbing and not-so-kind remarks from various members of his department, he took action on the word of a psychic, having first been convinced of Armand's accuracy on multiple details of the case.

It was the correlation between PsiCom members and Armand which helped convince Sergeant Thomas that psychic input could be valuable in providing new leads to cases which had come to dead ends and, perhaps, in actually solving crimes. But the **differences** between certain parts of the psychics' input are fascinating from a research point of view and can, eventually, help in training detective/psychic teams to work effectively together. For PsiCom had come up with perceptions of a lonely, despondent woman. Armand, on the other hand, had seen her as happy, excited and expectant. Since both sources gave valid information about Lucy Brady irregardless of their differing descriptions of her emotional state, where lies the answer?

A possible reason for the differences might be the PsiCom members were working from Lucy Brady's thimble, an instrument she used probably in her loneliest hours when she was alone, mending and sewing. When a woman is sewing, she is engaged in a routine, mechanical task, and in this state the subconscious mind can come close to the border of the conscious. While sewing and mending, Lucy Brady may have pondered her life — her weariness, discontent and lack of goals. It was probably emotions akin to these that the PsiCom psychics picked up.

Armand had worked with Lucy Brady's pink earrings, which she wore when she dressed up for social occasions and therefore they contained impressions of happier times. The last vibrations the woman had imparted to these favored baubles were filled with expectancy, excitement over a coming marriage, and the thrill of a precious secret she could soon share with her beloved sister.

Since, as Armand states, Lucy was hurrying to pack for a "second honeymoon," it is possible the last thing she'd be thinking of doing would be to sew and mend, and so her thimble did not contain any impressions of her recently revived happiness. The earrings **did**, and they told their story to Armand.

Lucy Brady, at the time of this writing, is still missing. If, as Armand declares, she was murdered in the southwest desert, her killer is still at large. However, Armand contends firmly, "The police know who did it. They just can't prove it — yet. But I know her body will be found, certainly by 1984. I keep seeing it, buried by that shack. When she's finally found, the case will be reopened. Perhaps then the man I **know** killed her will be brought to trial."

CHAPTER FOUR

"Psychic Detecting: Individuals vs. Groups"

Most reports of psychic detecting which appear in the public press involve individual psychics working with the policemen directly concerned with a particular case. However, there are **groups** now being formed in the United States which utilize multiple psychics, each contributing his/her impressions about the crime into a common pool of perceptions.

One advantage to the multiple method is that different bits of information are picked up by different members of the group. Therefore, the detectives may derive more information about each case. Another advantage is that, frequently, two or more group members receive similar pieces of information; this correlative factor may strengthen these bits of knowledge, making them potentially more valuable in solving the crime.

Armand became involved in multiple detecting in 1979 shortly after Sergeant Ed Thomas of the Overton Police Department contacted him on the Lucy Brady case. After Thomas had taped Armand's first reading on the case, he called in Mrs. Brady's son, Stan, to listen to the recording. Stan had been impressed by PsiCom's reading on his mother's disappearance; he was also intrigued by Armand's. Some time after Sergeant Thomas completed his interviews with Armand, Stan Brady himself corresponded with Armand, thanking him for his assistance and telling him of the correlations — and differences — between PsiCom's and Armand's own impressions on the case.

Armand learned that PsiCom had had considerable experience working with police from various communities near Los Angeles on cases of murder and missing persons. The five-member group were highly educated and held positions in the teaching, medical and psychological fields.

Armand was fascinated with the situation. His fascination lay in two main parts: first, that a **group** of highly trained and educated psychics were working with police in the Southern California area and, second, that the PsiCom members had visualized Lucy Brady as despondent and discouraged, whereas he himself had received the impressions from her jewelry that she was excited and even happy-go-lucky.

He **felt** his impressions of Lucy Brady's emotional state were valid, at least up to the time she had fondled the pink earrings trying to decide whether to take them with her on her honeymoon. Did PsiCom's impressions of despondency and despair come from "another source?" Stan Brady had mentioned that the Director of PsiCom, Louise Ludwig, held a Ph.D. in psychology, and Armand felt he could learn something from her group.

"I felt I sure would like to know her," Armand recalled later. "If she did this kind of work, maybe she could help me make my sensitivity better or improve on my ability or show me if I was going about it the right way, because I was more or less just doing what came naturally to me."

He told Sergeant Thomas that he wanted to meet Dr. Ludwig, and Thomas laughed. "I've spoken to her about the Brady case since Stan Brady requested PsiCom to participate in the investigation. He told her how impressed he was with **your** reading and Dr. Ludwig wants to know how **you** do it!"

Apparently there was some sort of mutual admiration society forming here. Armand got Dr. Ludwig's phone number from Sergeant Thomas and called her at Los Angeles City College, where she was a professor in the psychology department.

Louise Ludwig was pleased to received Armand's call. A few days previously she had received a letter from Stan Brady describing Armand Marcotte as a gifted psychic. Dr. Ludwig and Armand made plans to meet and discuss their mutual interests.

In this way, a series of sessions began; Armand drove the sixty miles to Los Angeles in order to work with the PsiCom group. He shared with them his method by which **he** received impressions about crimes — the fact that he felt he could **connect** with a murdered person's spirit by working with a piece of metal jewelry or some other item which had been closely associated with that person in life or which, ideally, had been on the person or in the immediate surroundings at the time of death. He explained his method of partially allowing the murdered person's spirit to speak through him, while at the same time he maintained rigid control of his mind.

PsiCom in turn, informed Armand how each of their individual psychic talents had been developed and told of their interest in developing a scientific methodology for police/psychic participation. They explained how they carefully taped each session they gave for police participants. Although they were under the same seal of secrecy as Armand was, they tried to encourage the detectives with whom they worked to "feed back" information as to which perceptions they provided were accurate and helpful. PsiCom desired to document whenever possible, for documentation is the heart of the scientific method. It is only through verified evidence that science will eventually take notice of the validity of the psychic methodology in police work.

For several months Armand and the PsiCom team worked effectively together, sharing information and subsequently improving their mutual skills. This exchange between the natural, untutored psychic and the scientific team was a fascinating phase of Armand's life.

"The more I did of police work, the more I decided that I wanted to continue in it," states Armand. "I made it known to the police departments who contacted me that I was available at any time. Dr. Ludwig encouraged me and she was very interested in following any of the cases I would work on."

"On several occasions I was asked to go to different areas, like El Centro, and was flown there by sheriff's departments. I would call Dr. Ludwig, and she would come out to Hesperia, and they'd pick us up at the Hesperia Airport and fly us to these various sites.

"In this way we were able to put things together much easier, she and I, because she was very intuitive, just like I was. What I missed, she picked up, and vice versa. We became sort of a team working with the police. Naturally, she wanted to bring in the other members of PsiCom and so when she'd get a case I would work with the whole group. If I'd get a case, I could bring her only, due to the problems of traveling."

It was an intriguing team — the natural, uncomplicated psychic and the inquiring scientist. But the police with whom Armand worked regularly began to balk at the arrangement. Due to the strict legalities of police work, the detectives were not permitted to share certain information and often lacked time to provide the documentation PsiCom requested. When working alone with Armand, they could encourage him during the sessions by indicating when "he was on the right track" and verify **some** details of a crime when they wished to elaborate on some particular point. But they seldom shared with Armand any **specifics** on how his readings had been of use to them.

It was not the detectives' fault. They **had** to work this way, because evidence by which crimes are solved becomes a matter of law and is, therefore, privileged. Since in most cases it is many months or even years before some suspects are brought to trial and convicted, the data pertaining to each case must remain locked up from public view.

This was the reason the detectives with whom Armand worked (and is still working) rarely came back to him to verify his perceptions and to inform him specifically on which areas he had been able to assist them. The only way Armand could tell that he had really helped was that the same detectives kept coming back to him seeking help on **other** cases.

Some of the detectives might have been willing to share, on a confidential basis, more specifics of a case where Armand had been of help, but the nature of police work again prevented this. Crime, as we all know, is rampant, and law enforcement officers are greatly overworked. There was simply no time to allow detailed feedback.

Armand accepted this situation. He was glad to assist any way he could, and this was the way it had to be.

PsiCom, on the other hand, had been established not only to assist police through freely available psychic consultation, but to establish a scientific methodology. This would involve published papers in scientific journals. Even though PsiCom respected the necessary seal of confidentiality, the detectives often had to decline the group's requests that they pinpoint areas in which psychic information had been of help, due to the legal and time problems involved. Even though the specific psychic impressions were followed out by regular police methods, and even though **proof** of guilt was obtained in the usual manner (though working from psychic clues) courts might frown on the source from which the information had originated.

There was another problem. Some of the detectives were asking Armand **if he could teach them his methods of psychic perception.**

Since Armand's talents were free-flowing and natural, his intellectual understanding of the process was incomplete. Although of superior intelligence, his formal schooling was limited, and he felt inadequate to instruct those detectives who wished to be taught. Instead, he would refer them to Dr. Ludwig, explaining her scientific background and advanced educational achievements.

PsiCom was setting up planned sessions for such instructions, but the detectives in Armand's area who regularly worked with him resisted the idea. If Armand wouldn't or couldn't teach them, they wanted to work with him alone.

Dr. Ludwig and Armand remain good friends, meeting often to exchange information, methods, ideas and theories. He values her advice and guidance, in particular her suggestions on how to present the subject of psychic talent to the general public in his lectures, his radio show, and to various media persons who seek him out for interviews. He values her as a professional, a talented psychic and a strong friend.

At one point Armand considered going back to school and obtaining an advanced degree in psychology so he could feel he was on the same educational level as Dr. Ludwig and her group. However, there were two factors in his life which persuaded him that this was unnecessary and, perhaps, even unwise. For one thing, he has a conviction that his life will not be too long. Aged fifty at the time of this writing, he expects to pass over onto the other side within the next decade, and he does not want to waste any time pursuing courses of study not directly related to his psychic work. Any advanced degree would involve many such courses. Secondly, he has been persuaded through conversations with detectives he works with, and by Dr. Ludwig herself, that his natural talent should not be tampered with. Trying to mold his ability to fit scientific models and theories would intellectualize it far too much. The result might be that he would become confused, doubtful or nontrusting of his own talents.

There are many kinds of psychic perception. It comprises a spectrum, on one end of which are abilities like Armand's and on the other, the more systematically trained methods like those of Dr. Ludwig and the other PsiCom members. Each psychic must work with the perceptions with which he or she feels most comfortable, and in the most relaxed setting.

Armand managed to continue working with PsiCom in another way. Periodically, the members of PsiCom hold workshops, sometimes for law enforcement personnel and sometimes for the general public. The most recent one (at time of writing) was held on Saturday, June 19, 1982 at the Spring Valley Country Club in Victorville. It was devoted to three specific areas:

(1) PSYCHOMETRY (psychic reading from personal objects);
(2) PRECOGNITION (perception of future events); and
(3) PAST LIVES THERAPY (Issues and research).

All of the PsiCom associates, like Dr. Ludwig, have advanced academic degrees and were engaged in professional teaching positions.

They were Dr. Shirley Barker, Dr. Ora M. Hook, who, like Louise Ludwig, were psychology professors, and Nancy Ramsey, M.S. an instructor of nursing. Armand participated as Special Consultant and Professional Clairvoyant. In workshops like these, both natural psychics and scientifically minded sensitives can merge their talents for the public good. Also, members of the public who wish to train the psychic talents which exist potentially in every human person can learn which methods can best help them achieve their goals.

Armand is not only psychically perceptive; he also has a sharp, logical understanding of human nature. In his usual unassuming manner, he described the dilemma faced by some policemen.

"As long as they [the detectives] came to me as an isolated psychic, they could wipe me out and ignore me. But when I brought in the scientific feel of it through PsiCom, they resisted it. When a few of them asked 'Do you ever give lessons?' I'd say that Dr. Ludwig was holding classes, and they didn't like that idea because here was a person who represented academic degrees and authority in the field.

"Then they'd think, if they were going to turn their jobs to **that** different area, they would have to go higher in school to do what they were doing. By bringing in the psychics with academic degrees, some detectives get a little nervous, thinking that some day in the future they might have to get some type of degree in psychology or parapsychology in addition to their studies in police science and criminology.

"The way I see it, this is the barrier between the policeman and the psychic. It isn't that they're **disbelieving** of psychic abilities. Many **do** believe that psychic talents exist, but at the same time the changes it would bring about make them uneasy.

"Using a psychic like myself without an education is to their advantage, but using a psychic with advanced degrees scares some of them off. They think the public might think a highly educated psychic was superior to a good policeman. Now Louise wouldn't ever give that impression because she's truly down-to-earth and very modest about her fine abilities, but some psychics might not be so generous.

"But it's still not so much the psychics looking down on the police, but that the **public** might look down on the police and look **up** to the psychics."

In actual fact, according to Armand, this dilemma is not based on reality. Although Armand feels the freeing of psychic abilities is part of man's evolutionary process, the abilities of detectives are still unique. They are schooled and trained in methods of crime detection and the scientific gathering of evidence which will hold up in court to bring about the conviction of criminals. These abilities are special and **apart** from the abilities of psychics who work with them to solve violent crimes.

The detective works in a purely physical world involving a physical crime and material evidence. The psychics, with their ability to perceive beyond our normal, physical space-time, bring an added dimension to crime detection. One will never replace the other; the detectives' jobs are quite secure. In Armand's opinion, until the human race is evolved enough to share psychic abilites freely and naturally, crime will remain a serious problem.

The psychic is an informal (and temporary) partner in the crime-solving business. The problem is how to admit the value of psychic talents and use psychics **publicly** without fear of ridicule or of jeopardizing the prosecution of criminal cases.

Armand believes these problems should be left for the public to decide. He envisions a future, not too many years off, when psychics will be used freely in police work. There will be no fear as to where the information came from which solves a crime. If a psychic has given a **key** which solves a felony, that fact will be immaterial. The important thing will be this: that a vicious criminal has been taken off the streets. Armand feels that eventually this open climate of acceptance will come through people like Dr. Ludwig and the other members of PsiCom.

"Dr. Ludwig is very good with people," states Armand. "She's the type that will bring this into reality — a compromise between the psychic and the detective. Eventually this type of police work will be a precise science. It will help bring about an understanding of natural psychic talents as well as trained psychic talents. And the two types of talents will accept one another on a high level of professionalism. Academic degrees won't enter into it.

"I think of Dr. Ludwig and the other members of PsiCom as very intelligent psychics of higher learning, and she thinks of me as a psychic who has natural ability. With people like her interested in people like myself, it can become a science because of her strength and ability to foresee things."

Dr. Ludwig was interviewed during the writing of this book. She is an intelligent, cordial woman whose soft blond curls frame a vivacious face. She was happy to contribute her ideas and experience, and gave the following formal, written statement:

During the three years that I have known Armand Marcotte I have consulted him about unsolved crimes brought by various law enforcement agencies to PsiCom and, in addition, have worked with him on cases brought directly to him by other agencies.

In both instances his strongest asset proved to be his ability to provide very detailed information, such as specific motives of suspects, location of previously undiscovered physical evidence, the importance of previously discarded evidence, sequence of events leading up to the crime, the actual events during the crime, idiosyncrasies in the physical or personality makeup of the suspect and/or victim, descriptions of (locations, houses, automobiles) and names or initials of suspects.

The quantity and quality of the information he has generated have been very impressive and, more to the point, have proven useful in the investigation of crimes.

Since 1975 I have worked actively toward the goal of helping psychics and police personnel understand each other so that effective use of reliable psychics such as Armand can become an accepted procedure available to law enforcement officers everywhere. In these days of high crime rate and lowered police budgets, it is my sincere desire that many will join Armand and myself in the successful pursuit of this goal.

/s/ Louise Ludwig, Ph.D.
President, PsiCom

November 1, 1982

Dr. Ludwig was not even aware that someone like Armand existed before Stan Brady contacted PsiCom in November 1979 in the hope of locating his missing mother.

Besides the correct information regarding Lucy Brady's appearance, home and her depression and ill health, PsiCom came up with other correct impressions about her: that she was interested in psychic activities and read astrology literature; she believed she was going to die soon; she wore a small watch on her left wrist and preferred flat-soled sandals, liked to sew and crochet, and wanted to revisit her childhood home. They also perceived that she had problems with her right arm from a stroke, had two sons, was weary of her surroundings and complained a lot.

Some other impressions perceived by members of PsiCom regarding Lucy Brady were incorrect, for no psychic or group of psychics gives one hundred percent accurate information in spite of claims to the contrary. An exceptional psychic, on an exceptional day, may approach eighty to eighty-five percent.[2]

At the time Stan Brady came to PsiCom for help, the group was working with private individuals as well as with representatives of law enforcement agencies. Now, however, they have a policy of working with bona fide law enforcement sources only due to the difficulty presented by relatives who are emotionally involved in the crime.

"Mr. Brady and I worked out these readings, and I gave him the results," states Dr. Ludwig. "He took them to Sergeant Ed Thomas of the Overton Police Department, who was assigned to the case. Later, Brady told me Sergeant Thomas had asked if it would be OK if he consulted another psychic on the case, because he'd heard about a "French Canadian up in the [California] desert" who was pretty good, and that Brady had told him, 'Sure, go ahead. Anything that will help, please do it.' I asked Mr. Brady to procure a copy of the taped reading by this other psychic if he could, as we would like to check ourselves and compare what we'd gotten.

"I gave the transcript of our reading to Mr. Brady, and Armand Marcotte read it. It was then that Armand first called me. After that we worked together on many cases — an ongoing relationship."

PsiCom had started as an informal group composed of persons interested in the field of psychic research. For a few years they met weekly, though informally, working out techniques to explore their possible talents for psychometry and precognition. Their approach has always been scientific; careful records were made of hits and misses and statistical accuracy charted.

They did not involve astrology, numerology or other forms of so-called "occult" aids in their studies. None of the members had studied any of these methods or had interest in them. They considered them unnecessary, and even undesirable, in their study. Applied parapsychology is becoming a science, and impressive work is being done in the field using the so-called "remote-sensing" or "remote-viewing" power of the mind without the aid of palmistry, astrology, tarot cards, etc.[3]

Dr. Ludwig accepts the fact that Armand feels he works with spirits, but the members of PsiCom do not feel that their psychically perceived information comes directly from spirits.

"Our methods of working are different, even within the group," Dr. Ludwig explains. "One of our members 'sees'; she has clairvoyance. Another one seems to 'hear' a lot of things, like a conversation, or bits of conversation, or names of cities or people. Another member, if she's been working on a case, during the next two or three nights she may have very vivid dreams that relate to the case. Sometimes another member will write on a PsiCom record sheet what she calls a 'nice fantasy,' because it feels that way at the time, but the information comes very spontaneously; then a lot of it will turn out to be really quite accurate. So, we get our information from different sense modalities."

The specialized sense modalities which give information to the various PsiCom members are not **exclusive** to each. It is simply a situation where some of them are more accurate with certain kinds of perceptions. For instance, two members perceive names that prove later to be accurate, and that is, traditionally, a difficult thing to do. They do not do it all the time — just occasionally. The names (of the murderer, for example) might be heard within the psychics' heads or they may see the name as in a vision or just **feel** it come without really experiencing it.

PsiCom members also do not usually envision the crime in progress, as Armand does. If they see the victim in their minds, it's usually after the person is dead. They can describe how the victim was found, and what the wounds were or how the victim died. But they **do** see the suspect (or whom they consider the suspect) and can describe his appearance and usually come up with the motivation.

The different methods and ways in which psychics receive their impressions — from various channels — is highly interesting to the scientifically-minded Dr. Ludwig. She points out that various psychics have differing philosophies about what they do. However, it is only the information which can be documented that will build a psychic/detective methodology.

The fact that psychics have differing philosophies regarding their own talents lies at the very heart of the skepticism with which many detectives regard them. Police need to be totally objective toward a psychic's stated philosophy. If he speaks of communicating with spirits, for example, it should make no difference to the inquiring officer **how** the information comes so long as the perceptions prove accurate and helpful. It is this total objectivity which is lacking in many law enforcement officers and causes many to regard psychics as "weird" or "cranks."[4]

To return to the interview with Dr. Ludwig, the situation regarding the thimble vs. the pink earrings (as psychometric objects) was explored with her. Dr. Ludwig explained that, in using the thimble, the perceptions of despondency and despair meant that the group's members were possibly tapping into another source for their information — a source different from which Armand perceived Lucy Brady's happy and excited state through the pink earrings.

"You can have as many different approaches to the problem as psychics you can talk to, actually," explained Dr. Ludwig. "We could have been tapping in at various levels of her awareness. Maybe consciously she felt she was happy, and we tapped into her unconscious depression, or it could be the other way around. Or we could have been tapping into a different period of her **life** than Armand was, so you would get a different reading as far as psychological factors go. For example, if you were describing her physical appearance when she was young, that would be obvious to her son, and if you were describing her as she was, close to the time of her disappearance, that would be obvious, too. But psychological factors — that could mean conscious or unconscious."

The hypothesis regarding the thimble/pink earring situation (as set forth in Chapter Three) was discussed with Dr. Ludwig. She felt that this was a possible explanation but that any other hypothesis could just **as** likely be the correct one.

Dr. Ludwig explained the details of her own philosophy regarding her own psychic talent. "My feeling is — I have no proof of this, other than my own subjective experience — but my feeling is that we sometimes switch into another 'channel,' if you want to use that expression, or get into some kind of altered state where at least **part** of the desired information is accurately available.

"Other parts of it are **not** accurate because of interference from our own logical minds. We try to keep analytical overlay out of our sessions, but that's the key struggle always — to keep your logical mind out of the way while you're trying to do this other kind of task.[5]

"It's not a deep trance, and sometimes it feels to me as though it's a different state, or a somewhat altered state, and sometimes it doesn't. And sometimes when I think I'm absolutely wrong and just 'making it up,' it turns out to be right. It's hard to say. It's a very ephemeral, transitory and hard-to-describe state and even difficult to identify whether you're actually in this altered state or not.

"Some of us, when we see what we **do** see, sometimes perceive these things as pictures that are inside our minds," she states. "And sometimes they are pictures that are **outside**. Then it's like looking at a movie screen, or the blank wall across the room."

Dr. Ludwig believes that psychic talent is just that — a talent, like a talent for music or singing or mechanical ability. If a person has **no** talent for, as an example, playing the piano, he can still learn, but progress will be slow, awkward and minimal. **Real** talent for music can lie dormant or it can be developed and bloom fully with comparative ease. In the same way, the psychic potential of each individual, whether it be small or great, will respond to proper training methods.

"I had been interested in psychic research for a long time in a casual way," explains Louise Ludwig. "I certainly never considered **myself** as psychic. After I received my M.A. in psychology, I called up Marjorie Kern, who at the time was the chairman of the Southern California Society for Psychical Research. I became a member of that group for several years and acquired a lot of background through reading and through acquaintance with people in that field. I learned theories and various types of experimental methods. People started coming to me and asking questions about it, because I could tell them what the scientific community had to say about different types of paranormal experience and suggest references for them to study.

"During this time, I had no interest in developing any talent I might have had. But then a small group of us began practicing with simple experiments. One of us would bring the name of somebody in an envelope, and we'd all try to perceive impressions about that person. The one who'd brought the name and **knew** that person would give us feedback immediately, and we'd keep records of hits and misses. Finally, I realized we had a group of several people who definitely had psychic talent — because I had verified their perceptions for myself. I started training them with other advanced exercises, and I'd do the exercises, too. Finally, we decided we **all** had talent.

"We worked a lot with psychometric objects. Each week, for years, one of us would bring an object that belonged to somebody only **they** knew. As we each psychometrized the object, we'd write down our impressions silently and independently. Then the person who'd brought it fed back information on it. Getting feedback immediately in this type of training session is necessary and very very helpful.

"Working with actual objects was much more fruitful than card-guessing or those types of mechanical experiments. There was more content, perhaps more emotion, related to an object that had been connected to a living, active person. The fact that a psychometric object is connected to a **personality** makes it much more interesting to a psychic.

"During the first couple of years we were doing this, we discovered:

(1) that our output increased, that is, we perceived more and were willing to speak more about what we felt; and
(2) in some categories we didn't seem to improve our accuracy — such as the traditionally difficult task of perceiving names — but in such things as the age and sex of the persons and their physical descriptions we did become more accurate."

During these first two years, the experiments were strictly for the benefit of the members of the group themselves. As Dr. Ludwig advises, developing one's own psychic talent to the maximum degree possible takes much effort, time and practice. This fact stops many persons from perfecting what might otherwise prove to be an important contribution to society.

Dr. Ludwig was asked if she felt groups were better in police work than individual psychics.

"I think sometimes groups that have worked together compatibly for a long time and know each other well, possibly might give a more comprehensive picture," she replied. "But I think there are many psychics, working individually, who are very good. I don't think it really matters. You're not going to get more accurate information or a greater amount of accurate information from a group or a single individual. I think it varies strictly with the group and with the individual.

"If you're after correlations — if several PsiCom members all agreed on some aspect of the crime — it could be that perception was right and that's why we picked it up. It also could be that we're reading each others' minds, or picking up on the mind of the detective, for instance, who brought the case to us. It might just mean that **somebody's** broadcasting on a stronger level. You have to be careful of that.

"We personally ask that inquiring law enforcement agencies send us a police officer who doesn't know anything about the case. Theoretically, if we work with someone like that, we won't be reading **his** mind and telling him back what he already knows."

She points out that there can be many complications in police/psychic teamwork. In her opinion, the only way she can ever know any information is accurate is after you've checked it out in reality, in the physical world. For this reason, she requests documentation and feed-' back from police departments with which they work, but more often than not the requests cannot be granted, for reasons of legalities and lack of detectives' time — the same reasons Armand himself does not receive much feedback. But aside from the police inability or aversion to providing feedback, law enforcement agencies do not seem to have a preference whether the psychic source is a group or an individual.

"When they, the police, are willing to ask a psychic for help, they're desperate, and they'll cooperate in any way that isn't completely outlandish. If you have to perceive information standing on your head, that's fine, if the information turns out to be accurate and helpful."

There are those things, however, that policemen **do** care about when looking for psychic sources, and with good reason:

(1) that the source can maintain confidence on a professional level, for any publicity about a case could sway a juror's mind;

(2) that the psychics are not using the police experience for their own personal gain, that is, to build up their own reputations; and

(3) that the cases are not compromised with the courts, since there is always the possibility that a judge might rule certain evidence "inadmissible" if he feels it was obtained without "probable cause," that is, on the word of a psychic.

According to Dr. Ludwig, some psychics have been guilty in the past on the first two points above. However, she was eloquent in her defense of the third point concerning "probable cause."

"A lot of people think that the psychic says to the police, 'The person that did that murder last week is named Joe Jones, and he lives at 7575 Fishtin Boulevard, and he's there from 5:00 to 7:00 every night eating dinner, so why don't you go and arrest him?'"

"That's not the way," Dr. Ludwig emphasizes. "Psychics **rarely** produce evidence that is admissible in court. They can supply detectives only with new leads or urge them to pay attention to a bit of evidence they've overlooked, or provide motivation of the criminal, or urge them to requestion some suspects. In one of our cases one of the psychics said, 'You've questioned a woman in this case. Go back and question her again, because you didn't get all the information you needed.' The detective went back and found out he **hadn't** gotten all the information because she didn't **know** it at the time he first questioned her, but the second time around he got the information he needed. Now that's not admissible in court but it did help that particular detective with that case."

"Even in those rare exceptions where a psychic provided information that is admissible in court, it still has to be verified in the physical world. Psychic impressions themselves are not admissible in court. They do **not** provide what could be considered 'legal evidence.' "

When it comes to requesting search warrants or arrest warrants on evidence derived from psychics, most judges will rule that a psychic's information is not probable cause. However, in one landmark case in Southgate, California, a psychic helped a police artist produce a drawing of a suspect she felt had murdered a child. On the strength of the parents' identification from the drawing, a suspect was arrested, and he eventually confessed to that murder and two others. The legal question here: was the psychic's perception sufficient to give the police probable cause to go after this particular suspect? The judge in the case ruled that the use of the psychic in this case was a valid investigative tool and that the suspect's arrest was legal.[6]

Dr. Ludwig applauds landmark cases like this, but she does not think the psychic/detective teamwork method will be accepted by starting with the judges. She is convinced it has to start with training police officers, which is what PsiCom is all about. We will hear more from Dr Ludwig, and from Armand Marcotte, on specific techniques of training — both for officers and psychics who might be interested in this field — in the last chapter of the book.

CHAPTER FIVE

"Armand's Psychic Techniques"

Ask any number of genuine psychics the question: how do **you** retrieve the information psychically from your mind? You most likely will receive differing answers from each respondent, as was amply demonstrated during the interview with PsiCom's Louise Ludwig.

Paranormal talents are not well understood; the actual source or sources of psychic perceptions is unknown at present, at least it has not been empirically demonstrated through scientific methodology.

Armand defines the "source" in terms comparable to the Supreme Intelligence our Western world calls God. He believes that he has lived in past lives and, in the course of evolution of his soul, that the spirit which is **himself** has evolved fairly high on the spiritual ladder. He feels his psychic talents are linked with this spiritual evolvement and explains that an evolved soul, being closer to God, can reach out to the Source and retrieve information which is not so readily available to a person unaware of God or of the process of spiritual evolution.

Armand has been aware of his psi faculties since age four or five. He believes everyone has at least the potential for psychic perception but that most persons, by reason of upbringing and formal education, are dissuaded from believing that such faculties exist.

Armand's mother was frightened by his ability to foresee events and to sense details of people's lives about which he, logically, knew nothing. She took him to a priest at an early age: the good padre tried to convince him that he was just "imaginative."

Armand knew better. He tried for years to hide his perceptions from his family but meanwhile allowed his mind to open up to the natural flow. But he had no understanding of what made him different from his friends. He was considered by them a "freak," but he considered himself normal.

Upon joining the Navy at the age of nineteen, he lost his reluctance to tell others about his cognitions. He still did not understand how the faculties worked, or what they were, but he was encouraged, from feedback by persons whom he "read," that his perceptions were accurate.

At the beginning of his naval service, Armand was a deckhand on a destroyer, then worked as a baker, a position which he held until his discharge four years later. By that time he had achieved the rank of third-class petty officer.

During this time, his destroyer, the *Kepler*, docked at an Indian port where it stayed for about three weeks. India fascinated him. He had planned to go there some day if he could ever afford it, and here he was, in this strange but intriguing land.

Whenever he had time off, he went sightseeing, and these excursions invariably took him down a certain street. At the end of this street was an Indian whom Armand refers to as a "holy man." He befriended this man, exchanging casual conversation, and often brought him small delicacies from the ship's galley. After several days of brief meeting, the Indian man said to him, "I see a golden cross over your head. Could I tell your future?"

Armand responded, "Sure. What do you want to know?

"He asked me the date and time of day I was born, and told me to come back tomorrow," states Armand. "The next day I went, and he told me within two weeks I'd be fighting a war. Then Korea broke out, and it was everything like he'd said.

"He also told me my life would change, and it did — drastically — after I came out of the service. He told me other things, too, all of which came true." At last, Armand could put a label on what had made him different from other people. Armed with a growing awareness and understanding, he visited Indian temples and learned about reincarnation. His experiences at these places of worship and continued conversations with "holy men" convinced him that reincarnation — involving positive and negative *karma* — was an actual fact and part of the Cosmic plan of the Creator.

He also refined his technique for "traveling in time," which is crucial to his work with the police, and which will be described in detail a little later in this chapter.

Returning to North America, he settled in Hesperia, California, and opened up a cosmetology school in Upland. He found the work relaxing; stress was minimal in this setting, and the resulting tranquillity aided the natural psychic flow. Gradually, through word of mouth, his ability became known as he informally gave readings for his clients and friends. He began holding small classes in his home for persons interested in psychic subjects, for Armand had discovered that he was not only a clairvoyant but a natural teacher as well.

None of his Indian studies were in actual schools or classes. The three-week visit of the *Kepler* to that Indian port precluded that, but he attained a considerable degree of self-education during the subsequent days after the holy man told his future. He had been advised to study astrology, and when his military service ended, he took a correspondence course with the Rosicrucians. He studied it properly and mathematically. When using it in readings at the present time, however, the astrological aspects of his readings are derived through his subconscious rather than any in-depth study of any particular person's birth date. By referring to his books on astrology, he psychically perceives the good and bad astrological aspects of a person's past, present and future.

"It's like looking into the 'archives,' " states Armand. "When I look up the birth date and time of birth, it forms a link into that person and his or her time. Like when a detective comes and gives me the birth information on a murdered person, I control myself into that person's time, just prior to when they were killed. Then I can perceive details of what led up to the death.

"By using the books as reference, I feel I become more convincing and more convinced. I can reassure my vision, like double-checking it. You take a person that's very psychic; he's going to have his good days and off days. But if he knows astrology, that off day can be corrected, because astrology is the mathematics of what takes place in a person's life. It shows the pattern. That person has the free will to change the pattern — to make it good or bad — but the psychic person can actually **see** whether it's going to go toward good or evil."

Armand has a certain regimen of diet and meditation which keeps his psychic talents at their fullest. He eats lightly — a small breakfast and lunch, and a nighttime meal of fish or other seafood with salad and vegetables. He eats very little meat. He prefers natural foods and, in spite of his career as a baker in the Navy, avoids sweet desserts, preferring fruit, nuts and berries instead.

"I think eating light, natural foods keeps the body healthy, and if you don't eat much meat, your mind is much sharper. I think vegetables, especially celery, give me a stronger sensitivity than I would have otherwise.

"Then when I do psychometry, in the most important sessions — like for the police — I will eat very lightly for three or four days so that I actually feel hungry. In this state, I feel supersensitive, as if my own vibrations, rather than being held down to earth, have more of an upward motion, nearer to the spiritual vibratory world of the spirits from which I derive my information."

His meditation exercises are a means of deriving maximum relaxation "I usually start counting down from ten, nine, eight and so forth, and then when I've done the counting, I meditate a minute and then allow the forces to come through. Whatever thought that comes into my mind, I relay to the detective, or whoever has come to me for consultation."

Armand had become known in the community as an accomplished clairvoyant when a gentleman who was a professor in a local college approached him for a reading. A skeptic, this man hoped to prove Armand a fake. However, he was so impressed with the psychic's perceptions that he decided to conduct an experiment. He sent about twenty of his students to Armand over a period of two years and later determined statistically that the psychic was at least eighty percent accurate in his readings. As parapsychologists are aware, eighty to eighty-five percent accuracy is very high — even the most famed of tested psychics hover around the same figure.

Encouraged by this experience, Armand made a decision. He would devote his life to a career as professional clairvoyant. He realized that many persons can be aided by consultation with skilled counselors, but since he was able to guide persons with problems by looking into their **future,** as well as their present and past, he would be able to help his human brothers and sisters in God — for Armand believes that all life is linked together on the Cosmic level.

Armand doesn't simply predict the future for clients. He usually sees two paths that can be taken and the consequences of both; he lets the client choose her or his destiny.

"One day a girl came to see me," relates Armand. "I felt death all around her. I told her this, and she confirmed she was in a state of depression. I counseled her to hold on through this state and not permit herself to be alone. I assured her the depression would be temporary. I could see she had a brilliant future ahead of her in the medical field."

A tape recording had been made of the session, which the young girl took away with her. Three weeks later she committed suicide. The policemen who investigated the death found the tape and contacted Armand for more information. He remembered the girl and told them what he knew. Later her mother came to see him; he states he knew it was her mother even before she told him. Compassionately, he recalls her grief; if her daughter had just held on, she would have had a bright future.

As far as **specific** techniques of giving a reading are concerned — to private citizen and to police alike — Armand must first completely relax his mind. He does this best in his own familiar surroundings — his home and his office — for there the vibrations are attuned to his mind and are like an extension of himself. Inharmonious vibrations from strangers, unaccustomed loud noises and the like are kept to a minimum. In this way, he can better tune in to the vibrations of the individual who comes at the appointed time seeking help.

Armand, in making appointments for private readings, asks only the phone number of the client (in order to be able to reach them if the appointment must be postponed), and sometimes their first name. He prefers to know nothing about them before seeing them, but asks them to bring a personal object, preferably metal, which is intimately associated with them. He also asks their birth date at some time during the session.

He works basically the same with policemen on crimes, but here he wants to know if the victim of the crime was male or female, the date of disappearance or death, as well as the birth date; he also requests that the detective bring an item of clothing or jewelry belonging to the victim, preferably something that was on their person at the time of death.

"When I look up the birth date and time, it's like a computer. It seems to formulate a person in my mind. I can see the form, at first indirectly. This form — the individual — moves about in many directions in my mind's eye.

"At first it's in flashes, a little like a flashlight being turned on and off. When I get a flash of the form and personality, I more or less put a slow-motion camera on it, and then my mind begins to shape like you see clouds. Then the clouds seem to disappear, and I can see clearly what has happened to this individual.

"It's a floating feeling, a very light feeling. My mind is light; it's like there's nothing there, but **all** this information comes. It's like I'm looking into a whole glass or pitcher of water that's going to be pouring out.

"Then the individual's life seems to run out from them. I keep going deeper into this, and I see myself floating above and looking into that part of their life that took place.

"Sometimes, as in a police case, I'm way ahead of the crime. Sometimes I'm way **behind** the crime, so that the detective has to say, 'That's too far back. We know **that** happened two years ago,' for instance. So I move myself into another Time span."

Armand's description of how the psychic faculty works for him is unique to himself. However, his statement of "floating in Time" fits neatly into one hypothesis which some psychic researchers have developed to try to explain how the psi faculty works — the idea of a pool of knowledge, existing somewhere in what some call the Cosmic Consciousness or Universal Mind, that theoretically contains all details of every human experience. It consists of data regarding each individual human being who has ever lived, or who **will ever live**, in our space-time continuum.[7]

This hypothesis has been partially confirmed by scientists who are experts in the fields of quantum mechanics and the quantum theory. Time, in other words, is an artificiality, invented by men's minds in order to perform satisfactorily in our physical universe. In actual fact, it is suspected that Time, as we know it, does not exist — but that all experiences, and all knowledge, exist in an eternal **now**.[8]

It is possible that psychics like Armand are tapping the eternal **now** when they pull out information about a particular individual without the use of any of their five ordinary senses. It is not known just how the object related to the person (the metal jewelry, etc.) helps the process. All Armand knows is that holding an object which the person used in life is sometimes necessary to extract valid information.

"When I'm holding onto something of theirs, the impressions get very strong. I like metal because it seems to hold imprints of a time span when this person was fully activated. Maybe it holds imprints better because metal is dense itself. But other objects, besides metal, hold the imprints also. It's just like, for instance, picking up a comb and using it; for those few moments the comb is alive because it's got motion to it. Then you lay it down, and it becomes dead. It's been an instrument for a little while.

"So if a person has a favorite ring, or watch, or brooch, they carry it around with them a long time. It's **alive,** imprinting what's going on, what happens to that person over a long period of time. I feel a **flow** through an instrument like this — the ring or whatever — and it all goes through my mind.

"Take another instance. I pick up a pencil; when I touch it, it carries my vibrations. When I lay it down, it's part of my past, and I keep going forward. But something like metal jewelry, or an item of clothing, that's on a person at the time of violent death — the whole thing becomes an impression of that scene. Then the piece of jewelry lies dormant.

"When a policeman brings me that piece of jewelry, I can revitalize it by handling it and tell you what happened on the scene of the murder up to the time the person died and the metal object became dormant."

His psychic impressions are received in different forms, and he receives differing perceptions with different individuals.

"Sometimes I hear words or sentences or noises," explains Armand. "In other cases I see events like on television. With others it comes as flashes of thought. The thoughts come very fast. Then in other situations, I just **feel** that something is accurate, and that's **really** strange!"

In many cases, sensory input of various kinds combine to give a myriad of impressions. Then it is as if he is actually viewing the crime scene, hearing conversation, knowing what one or more of the participants are thinking, and, in addition, **feeling** added bits of information also. In those cases where he perceives what he feels is the actual spirit of the murdered person, all these forms of data are likely to be present.

"In some cases, the scene appears detail for detail," states Armand. "In other cases, the information creeps in, as it were, afloat from the back. It's hard to explain what I mean. For example in a case of a missing person, where I haven't been given an object that was on their person at time of death because their death isn't a proven fact, I pick up information from objects they've touched before they disappeared. In this way, I can determine what their mood was at about the time they disappeared, and sort of read from their minds what was going on in their lives. Then, clues can be given the detectives as to what was happening to them — things that nobody else might have known but which would give a lead to the circumstances under which they disappeared.

"Like in the case of Lucy Brady," he explained." When I touched that particular pair of earrings, I knew these were one of her favorite pieces of jewelry. Then I knew she felt happy and excited, and it was like I was reading her thoughts. I felt she was going to get remarried secretly and that's why she was going away. Then, later, I knew she was dead because I felt cold. I'd get flashes visually of her, later on, buried next to a shack in the desert.

"Sometimes I'm off in my times, especially when I don't have a metal object worn on the person's body at time of death. I **know** they'll find Lucy Brady's body, for example, for certain before 1984, but they haven't found it yet. I watch the papers for things like this, because I can be off in my time.

"Anyway, the impressions I discover about what took place during a crime come **when I throw myself into that time of the material I'm working with**. Anything we come in contact with is left with our imprint. That's why I prefer to work with a person's possession that other people haven't handled much. For example, a crime victim's ring would pick up various detective's vibes if they touch it a lot.

"It's most important in doing this work that I remain completely relaxed, completely afloat," Armand reiterates. "When I discover myself in the time zone I want, it's like I'm **everywhere** on the scene. Armand, **as I am myself** — a person with a body — isn't there, but my mind is there seeing the crime going on. It's like the victim's taking me by the hand, showing me what took place before they died.

"I don't close my eyes; I don't go into what they call a trance. My physical eyes are open, but I'm in a daze. I've had policemen say, 'Are you all right?' because sometimes I get very pale. When this happens, it's like I'm actually part of the victim and feel what they felt physically. On one case with the Border Patrol, I actually got sick, because that man really suffered before he died. My emotions went into that person, and it was awful!"

In most cases, however, Armand simply touches the object associated with the person, gets the proper vibrations, sees the person and moves on their Time track. He states that he knows when he's on the right track. If the detective says, "More," confirming that **he** knows Armand is on the right track, he pushes himself farther into the clouds surrounding the person's form to see the event and the results. Having completely cleared his mind of his own personality and problems, he describes it as floating above his physical form. He maintains control of his physical body in **real** Time, but the impressions he receives are coming through **his spiritual senses**.

"In other words, I'm in astral travel," Armand explains.' "I go above my head, completely out. When the spirits of murdered people come to me, I permit them partial use of my body, mainly the vocal cords, so they can tell what happened. In one case in El Centro, California, the spirit of a murdered Latino came through and spoke Spanish words and phrases, including the Spanish word for 'icepick.' The victim was telling what the murder weapon had been. Now, I don't speak Spanish, and I couldn't tell you to this day what the Spanish word for icepick is, but I said it then.

"These spirits who come are there because they're as anxious to get a crime resolved as we are. But ordinarily, common sense prevents the victim's relatives, friends and detectives from **listening** to them. The difference is, I allow them to guide me on a tour of what happened to them."

Armand receives the most valid information when he is in his own surroundings, as we have said, but also he is most accurate when he knows nothing about the crimes, the victims or his personal clients, not even full names. If he is aware of any reality concerning a crime, for instance, the data acts as "noise" hitting against his mind. Scientists are beginning to call this phenomenon "analytical overlay." It occurs when the intellectual left hemisphere of the brain starts to interfere with the intuitional data flowing into the brain's right hemisphere.[10] If some of the intellectual data seem logically inconsistent with what his faculties are telling him, the left brain is likely to try to "correct" the data. This is the bane of psychics and parapsychologists who study this subject. The information psychics perceive best are unintellectualized impressions — geometric shapes, colors, auditory sensations, motion, and raw visual data. Very few psychics are able to come up with valid intellectualized data such as names, exact directions and measurements.[11]

Another problem confronts Armand (and other psychics) who attempt to work firsthand out of their own environments. "When I am taken out to a crime scene without first "seeing" it psychically in my own relaxed atmosphere," states Armand, "there's a lot of unfamiliar noise that I call 'static.' Then I can get false information at times. It could be that some other spirits other than the murdered person might be trying to pose as the victim I'm trying to contact."

Since we hope this book can be a kind of preliminary manual for detectives and other psychics who wish to work together, and for the general public who want to know more about how this work is best done, **it is important to state that each psychic should be permitted to gather his first impressions about a case in his own way**. If he or she prefers to work first in their own surroundings to avoid analytical overlay and other interfering conditions such as distracting noises, and false vibrations, the detective should be willing to go along with their wishes.

"In my own surroundings, I do better because my guides are stronger and I can influence and hold onto my physical self so that other entities won't control and diversify my thinking. I can get wrong information at a crime scene because I see the actual scene on the physical plane, and my intellectual mind tells me, 'Well, **this** might have happened' and 'That might have happened.' I don't want any preconceptions as to what might have happened."

In working with private clients, Armand sometimes censors the flow of information he receives psychically. If he sees a tragic event in a person's near future, he will soften the information if he feels the person is not prepared to hear it.

"Awhile back, I read a young woman," he states, giving an example. "She was in the military and her husband was a doctor in the Air Force. I saw her husband dying in a plane crash, and it seemed like it was going to happen soon. I didn't feel she was ready to hear that. So I told her to tell her husband he should be very careful. That's all I would say about that, but I went on and told her she was going to inherit a lot of money this year and that she was going to lose someone close to her. Right off the bat she thought, 'That's going to be my mother in-law. She's seventy-nine and she's loaded!' I just let her assume what she wanted to. But at least I prepared her, in a way. I told her she wouldn't have to worry the rest of her life, and she won't because the 'inheritance' will be her husband's insurance. She left very happy, and when all these events start clicking off, she'll put two and two together.

"It wouldn't have been possible to tell her to warn her husband not to get on planes for the next few months, because he was in the Air Force and had to follow orders. But it was his destiny to die young. Like I was taught, 'there's a time to be born and a time to die,' and his birth date gave me the time his death was drawing near. I saw that in a past life he had committed suicide and that it was destined for him, in this life, that he would be taken out of the picture when everything was going great guns for him. That's the explanation for a lot of early deaths."

Armand, in working with private clients, averages seven or eight readings per day, but in working with detectives limits himself to two. Reliving tragic and violent events weakens him, and the very process of going back in Time is exhausting in spite of the relaxed state he enters. And, of course, he does not withhold any information he perceives when working with the police, as there are no personal emotional involvements, such as occur in private readings.

In crime cases, he uses the astral-travel technique more so than with private clients. Even so, much of his perception is symbolic, linked with raw visual imagery. Even in cases where the detective has provided him with the date of the victim's death, dates are inventions linked with the artificiality of Time and do not mean that much to the intuitional right side of the human brain.

"Timewise, the main way I can orient myself is with the seasons. For example, if I see a fallen leaf or an orange leaf, I know the crime took place in the fall. If there's no snow on the ground but rotten leaves, then it's late fall. If there's snow on the ground, it's winter.

"Likewise, if I see a large body of wavy water, then I know the crime took place by the ocean. If it's a large body of calm water, then it's a lake, or stagnant water, a pond. I see rocks and other identifying marks of the scene, and then I can describe the area where the body is. I don't think the spirit is **sending** me the visualizations — I just see them in their Timetrack.

"In communicating with the spirits of the victims, it's just like their lives are motion pictures. They can go back and pinpoint in their lives what you want to know. They say when a person dies, they review everything that they've done with their lives. It's like that. The spirit reviews everything and when I throw myself in there, they review **with me** what led to their deaths. They try to pinpoint the person or persons who killed them so they can meet their punishment. That way the criminal won't have to come back and face the same reality again."[12]

In Armand's own understanding of his psychic faculties, the phenomena known as astral travel, reincarnation, and negative *karma* are treated as established facts. Scientists are studying the apparent phenomena of astral projection and recurring lives but have yet to decide on firm theories regarding them. The idea of negative *karma* (necessity to pay for one's transgressions in successive lives) has not yet been tackled by science, but it seems closely linked with that of reincarnation. Until the psychic faculties are accepted generally by science, it is well to keep an open mind regarding the three separate phenomena Armand discusses above. They are part of his existence and linked with his successful career as a professional clairvoyant, and scientific validation of them might come sooner than we think.

The idea of a spirit reviewing their lives with Armand is not so strange either. Many reputable persons, who experienced near-death situations, have described how "their whole life flashed before their eyes." If the elan vital (life force principle) of the human person is, indeed, nonmaterial, it exists on a plane which is not restricted by our space-time. All the incidents of our lives could exist in an eternal **now** and be available to psychics who are contacting spirits while in **their** astral or spiritual forms.

Armand goes beyond the individual spirit's desire to see justice done. He sees a Cosmic interest in solving crime.

"It's God's way of bringing us to stop it," he states. "They (the victims) want us to stop it, because we all are part of God. And since crime is evil, God wants it to end, because evil is contrary to the Good, which is God. He wants the criminals to pay for their sins, but if they don't pay, they come back in another life and go through the same thing, until they get caught and pay for it."

The idea of *karmic* debt, although foreign to Western thinking, is strangely akin to the teaching of the Catholic Church on Purgatory. The Church teaches that a soul, upon death, if not purified enough to enter Heaven immediately, must spend varying amounts of "time" in a state of existence (Purgatory), which name is derived from the Latin word for "cleansing." The time spent in Purgatory, according to this doctrine, depends upon the magnitude and number of their sins. The Church does not definitively state just **what** Purgatory is, but describes it as a process by which we are purged of our residual selfishness so that we may become one with the self-giving God.[13]

It is possible that the Eastern idea of negative *karma* and successive lives (reincarnation) and the Western (Catholic) idea of Purgatory describe one and the same after-life process. No answer is possible at this time.[14]

It is also possible that the spirits of crime victims, especially those who are murdered violently, are not at peace and need to try to help bring their murderers to justice. Armand believes that in the after-life, emotions are muted. Hate, except in rare circumstances, is not present, nor are other negative emotions. Armand states that murder victims do not wish for revenge but seek to have their murderer's *karmic* debts resolved. In the after life, according to Armand and other talented psychics, spiritual qualities such as mutual love and charity predominate. Victims like "the man who hated pigs," Joe Casaneda, are rare.

"If they still hate their murderers, they're going to try to seek revenge **by forcing them to be born again, perhaps in order to be murdered themselves.** The victim has to face the fact of his death and wipe the slate clean. Those who want revenge are only destroying themselves; they can't go beyond to a higher level of spiritual existence until they learn to forgive.

"But we're all eventually going to have to go home to our Father, God, and we all have to evolve spiritually. We have to work to help one another reach that goal. And so, in doing this work, I'm helping them reach a higher plateau and state of spiritual evolution."

Scientific proof of Armand's interpretation of how his psychic talents work cannot, at this point in time, be presented. Other psychics describe differing processes to explain their faculties. But since Armand is an intelligent gentleman with finely honed psychic gifts, we can accept his word on how **he** thinks it works.

CHAPTER SIX

"Tidy Knots and Loose Strings"

There are two major problems confronting detective/psychic teamwork as it exists today. The first concerns the restrictions imposed by secrecy and legalities. Possible answers to this problem will be found in the last chapter of this book.

The second major problem is that the psychic methodology is used, if at all, only in cases where all leads have run out, all clues exhausted, and when a detective is desperate for help from **any** source.

Why should this be so, when there is excellent psychic talent available in most areas of the country — psychics who are willing to cooperate under the legal and ethical considerations necessary for this type of work? The main tragedy to date is that police, for many reasons, currently use psychics only as a last resort.

This chapter will help to demonstrate how **early use** of reliable clairvoyants can detect missing persons and prevent violence. The preceding chapters are necessarily based on partially verified information. We have, for example, our own transcripts of Armand's descriptions of details in each of the four murder cases we are free to use, and his own philosophy and explanations regarding his psychic abilities. But we do not, of course, have the tape recordings of Armand's sessions made by the detectives involved in these four cases. These recordings are part of the official records of these ongoing murder investigations. Public use of these would compromise these cases, if and when they eventually come to trial. In short, revealing police records about their use of psychics would fly in the face of common sense.

The cases below, however, are backed by signed affidavits of the principal witnesses who, because they are civilians, are not bound by the legal restrictions facing policemen. They prove Armand's strong clairvoyant abilities, however, and are backed by tape-recorded statements and transcripts in the authors' files. The names of the people involved and some of the cities have been changed to prevent unwelcome publicity.

In the spring of 1982, Mr. James Stockton, a resident of Montclair, California, made an appointment with Armand. Stockton was not interested in psychics and even less interested in having a personal reading. But his mother had gone to Armand shortly before and had been so impressed with what he had told her that she urged her son to see him, too.

Stockton, together with his partner, owns a trucking business in Ontario. He is a hard-headed, practical businessman whose company, although successful, had experienced some minor problems.

"My mother thought Armand was fantastic," James Stockton stated in an interview for this book. "You've **got** to go see him," she kept saying.

"So, more or less to keep her happy, I made an appointment one morning in early spring 1982. I can't even remember the exact date. He had no knowledge of me whatsoever. He asked only for my birth date and time of birth, which I had because I'd asked my mother beforehand. After I sat down by his desk, without any introductions, he said to me, 'You have three daughters.'

"I am married and have two daughters. I told him this, but Armand insisted, 'You have a third daughter.' She lives in another state, and she has light eyes and she's between twenty and twenty-two years old."

Stockton had been married previously more than twenty years ago, but this union had ended in divorce. Into this marriage a baby girl with light eyes had been born. Stockton rapidly searched his mind. He had not really kept track of how old this child would be, having remarried and all. He had not seen this daughter since she was six months old and had no definite knowledge of her whereabouts. A few weeks previously, he had happened to run into his former brother-in-law, his first wife's brother. In casual conversation, he learned that the baby girl he had last seen at age six months was living in Las Vegas. He had not acted on the information; it merged into his subconscious and was one of the things farthest from his mind when Armand mentioned his "third daughter with light eyes."

Then the psychic dropped a bombshell. "Within ninety days," he told Stockton, "you'll hear from this daughter. She'll get in touch with you."

He told Stockton that there would be hard feelings, in different ways, resulting from the visit; all of this, however, would be resolved. The hard feelings were not on the daughter's part, but stemmed from the maternal side of her family.

James Stockton didn't know what to make of this prediction. He continued to listen as Armand told him other facts about his life, all of which were accurate, and offered advice on two or three other matters. The session ended and Stockton left Armand's trailer puzzled.

"In about four or five weeks, I got a phone call," Stockton stated. "It was from this daughter, Livia. She wanted to come down to see me. She had married, she said, and was living in Las Vegas."

"I agreed I'd like to see her, too," continued Stockton. "She and her husband drove down to my place. I found out she was twenty-two years old. We had a very good visit. It was fantastic, the way it happened. I couldn't understand how Armand could have known, but it happened just like he said."

Livia had made up her mind to seek out her father and was acting on her own. Her mother and maternal grandparents knew nothing of her visit. Because Armand had predicted all hard feelings would be resolved, Stockton and his newly-found daughter, Livia Morely, expected everything to eventually work out well with her family.

After the reunion with Livia, Stockton returned to Armand for another appointment. The amazing prediction (or coincidence?) had begun to build in him a belief in Armand's psychic talents. He told the clairvoyant what had happened and showed him a picture of Livia. Armand was not surprised, only pleased. He was used to clients returning with validation of his readings.

Holding Livia's picture, Armand told Stockton that his daughter had had a miscarriage but that she would be pregnant again, soon. He also warned him to watch out for specific problems in his business; he forecast a slackening of income in the first part of October 1982, but reassured him that profits would start rising again in the remaining months of the year.

The statements about Stockton's business came true. He and his partner rode the waves and gradually business affairs straightened out. But on September 10, 1982 Stockton drove to Utah on a trucking haul. He stopped by Las Vegas to see Livia. She was delighted to have her visit returned and accompanied him on the ride to Utah. On the way, she confided that she had been pregnant but had had a miscarriage. No one except her husband and herself knew of this, for they had decided not to worry their families. She was awaiting the results of a medical test because she suspected she was pregnant again. Once more, Armand had been incredibly accurate.

"I sure believe Armand now, although I didn't when I first came to see him," states Stockton. "I hope that a book like this will sort of open up the field and show detectives that it's respectable to use psychics, if they are anything like Armand."

"The main thing, of course," he continued, "is that I've been able to establish a good relationship with my daughter after twenty-two years as a result of this. Armand is scary. He tells you things that aren't even on your mind. How can he bring out things by reading your mind if you're not even thinking of those things at the time?"

How, indeed? James Stockton's experience was just another example that Armand (and other talented clairvoyants) seem to tap hidden sources of information. They do not do this by simple telepathy (if telepathy between two individuals can be termed 'simple!'), but by delving into unknown reservoirs of knowledge.

How many "missing persons" could be located by anxious relatives if reliable psychic help were immediately available? Runaways could be distinguished from kidnap victims, and the agonizing twenty-four-hour waiting period forced upon families by overworked police could be eliminated. Lost children might be quickly found, and violent crimes against the young might be prevented.

The case of Jane Robertson is an even more startling example of Armand's abilities. But this time the clairvoyant did not merely perceive a reunion between a father and child but actually helped save a man from death. Jane Robertson, before visiting Armand for the first time, had an attitude of unbelief much like that of James Stockton. Although she had some minor experiences which seemed to be of paranormal origin, she did not believe in consulting psychics. But her sister-in-law, as well as the mother-in-law of one of her sons, had been to him and were intrigued by what he was able to tell them. They started to talk about the Fontana psychic and the news reached Jane.

As events he predicted for these two women came to pass, Jane began to wonder. This strong vital woman had five sons who were police officers and a daughter who was planning to enter the Academy in November 1982. Jane became interested in consulting Armand to see what he might pick up about the way her children's lives were going. She was a little afraid of what he might tell her; she didn't want to know if any deaths were going to occur among her children.

She made an appointment and then bought a small tape recorder. Her son's mother-in-law, during her own appointment, had made notes of the session, but regretted afterward not having recorded it. The night before Jane's appointment, she taught herself how to work the minicassette recorder, familiarizing herself with the controls. She recorded with it several times; each time it functioned perfectly.

She was ready, but in her own mind she did not really know why she was doing this. She felt strangely drawn toward the appointment, yet desired to cancel it. Her ambivalence kept her from sleeping that night.

The next morning, a hot August 30 in 1982, she showed up at Armand's office, still led by an unfamiliar guidance she had never experienced before. As usual, Armand had not asked her name and knew nothing about her. He had not been told of any connection with prior clients.

Jane Robertson didn't have anything specific to ask about any of her children, and since the appointment was only one-half hour long, she decided to let **him** do the talking. She said only one thing initially.

"If you see any deaths among my children, I don't want to know about it," she cautioned. Although she was not affiliated with any particular church, she had an inner spiritual faith. She felt that her nightly prayers for each of her children would keep them safe from mortal danger in spite of their hazardous professions.

But a strong feeling that he was going to tell her something she might not want to hear still lingered in her mind. She pushed the buttons on her minicassette to "Record" position and made sure that the reels were turning properly. Then she took out the list of her children's birthdays and times of birth and began feeding them one by one to Armand.

"I just want to know how each of their lives will be going," she ventured.

"When she first sat down before me," states Armand in an interview for this book, "I saw a crown on her head, full of stars. I guess that's the best way I can express it. To me, when I see a mother, I see her crown, and sometimes that crown is full of stars, and these are her children.

"I said to her, 'My God! You have a lot of people around you that are either in the police force or work around the legal department,' and she was impressed with that."

In general, the reading proceeded smoothly even though Jane's list was long. The majority of the children's lives would be fine, without major mishap, according to Armand. But he warned her about a son-in-law who was planning to buy a motorcycle to take him back and forth from work. He should not do this for at least six months, warned Armand, for he perceived a fearful freeway accident in which this son would be involved while riding a motorcycle. He also perceived that her youngest daughter would enter a new profession in November 1982 and excel at her work. This impressed Jane, for he was evidently "seeing" her daughter enter the Police Academy according to her plans.

Armand continued to go down the list as Jane gave him the birth date and time for each. Later, he explained the process (for purposes of this book) by which he obtained information on each of Jane's children.

"This crown full of stars I saw over her head," he states, "had each star glittering in a different light. I'd sort of go into each light, which is somehow synonymous with a person's aura, and pick up information. But one star I saw farthest away from her. It appeared to be tarnished, or not as brilliant as the others.

"It wasn't by **her** choice that he was farthest away, but by some dramatic thing that had happened in his life. When she gave me the birth information on this son, I went into this aura of light and pursued it in its time slot. I wanted to know why it wasn't as bright as the others. He seemed to be involved in law enforcement, and I perceived one of his comrades had been killed or wounded in a shootout. This shook him up; he couldn't handle it, and he'd had a nervous breakdown. I could see danger of death around him, strong — if he wasn't brought into her fold again.

"I felt that with the mother's love and understanding, and with that of his wife's, he could survive. He needed the feeling of being wanted, and I felt that he could be successful in another area, but that he should not follow a legal or police-type career.

"The tarnish was there on the light because his health was fragile. It was related to a lot of drinking, and I saw that he wasn't at his own home. I felt that death would **hit** him through self-doing, maybe by drinking too much or drinking the wrong kind of booze. I told the woman if she didn't go after him and bring him back that he would end up dead."

Jane Robertson grew alarmed but still maintained her normal skepticism. The half-hour session was passing by rapidly, and she still had other birth dates to give Armand.

"You get in touch with this boy!" advised Armand.

"I haven't seen him for a long time," protested Jane.

"Well, you get in touch with him **now** and tell him to be very, very careful," insisted Armand. "I don't know whether the danger is in his work or whether it came from some other source, but there's something there. He seems to be suicidal."

Jane thought she was getting all of Armand's reading on tape. What he was saying about this son, Terry, was alarming, but she decided not to pursue the subject. She still had questions about the rest of her children and their spouses. At the end of the session, however, Armand again said, firmly,

"You've **got** to get hold of that one! You **have** to get in touch with him! He's **got** to be warned because he's in so much **danger!**"

Listening to him, Jane's thoughts sped back over the past years of her son Terry's life. He was a police officer in Phoenix, and was married with children. He was in a high-pressure job plus having the responsibilities of supporting and rearing a family. He had married into a close-knit family; his in-laws lived near them in Phoenix. His wife was understandably distressed at his ever-mounting pressure and felt that he was somehow neglecting her. Her parents, trying to see that their daughter was not subjected to unhappy situations, added to Terry's problems.

He had briefly separated from his wife and took a leave of absence from the Phoenix Police Department. He moved back to Chino, California, to be near his parents and brothers and sisters, for there was a close bond of affection among these family members. He entered the Riverside Police Academy and began telephoning his wife nightly, trying to persuade her to bring their family out to California. Slowly, they patched things up, and she came out with the children for a visit.

Terry wanted to settle in Riverside, but his wife was closely attached to her own family. She refused to live permanently in California.

Terry went back with his wife and children to Phoenix. For eight years he had lived under tension there; now he was returning to the same pressures. Nevertheless, Jane had thought his difficulties had been straightened out. Realizing that family friction of any kind is harmful to young marriages, she resolved that she would not interfere in any way. She let it be known that if Terry's family could help in any way, they would be glad to have him call them; otherwise, they would leave him alone.

Months had gone by. In December 1981, Jane had spoken briefly to Terry's mother-in-law regarding her grandchildren's Christmas gifts and had been reassured that everything was all right with the little family. She again asked to be notified if anything went wrong and was assured this would be done.

Christmas passed. There was no response from Terry — no

thank-you for the children's gifts and no Christmas card. Mother's Day passed with no greetings from Phoenix. Jane continued to pray and made herself believe that Terry was doing well — until Armand insisted, "Your son is in terrible danger!"

Jane left Armand's office shaken and worried. She got in her car and turned back the tape in her recorder to the beginning. She set the machine on "Play," intending to relisten to the session as she drove toward her Chino home. Perhaps relistening could help congeal her confusion into a workable plan. She heard the "swish, swish" of the tape, but there were no traces of conversation — none of Armand's words, none of her own occasional comments. Frantically, she spun the tape back to the beginning and played it again. Not one word of the session had recorded.

"I got so shook up I don't know what happened to me," explains Jane. "My son Chet lives in Fontana, and I drove to his house to wait for him to come home from work. I got so hyper, and I'm not like that. I'm usually very calm — there's always an explanation for everything. But it blew my mind. I listened through the entire tape again, but there was absolutely nothing on it.

"Finally my son arrived home. He said, 'You look terrible! What's wrong?' I told him what the psychic had said, that Terry was going to be killed, and I let him listen to the empty tape."

Chet was disbelieving of psychics, but he realized that his mother was truly upset. He advised her to drive home and call Terry that night. Jane realized this was the only logical course to take.

When Jane called Terry that evening, he was not home, and she talked to Diane, his wife. Jane briefly explained her visit to the psychic and told Diane what he had said about the danger surrounding Terry. She deliberately did not tell her that Armand had mentioned suicide.

"Diane hesitated," related Jane. "Then she started telling me all these things that had happened. Four of Terry's fellow police officers had been recently killed. The last one was his partner. This final tragedy was more than Terry could take. He started drinking, and now the problem had progressed to the point where he would leave his home on his days off and stay intoxicated for two to three days at a time."

Jane phoned Terry at a number Diane gave her and spoke to her son. She told him what Armand Marcotte had said and asked him to promise he would be very, very careful.

"You know me well enough," she told Terry, "that if this thing wasn't just tearing me to pieces I wouldn't be calling. But I **know** you are in so much danger, and I've just got to tell you this!"

Jane could not tell whether or not her appeal had impressed Terry. He hesitated, then said he would call her back and hung up the phone.

A few minutes later Diane called Jane back.

"My God, what did you say to Terry?" Jane remembers Diane saying. "He's so upset he's crying and he told me to come get him. I don't know how to tell you this, but Terry tried to commit suicide awhile ago. He put a hose through the car and flooded it with carbon monoxide. We got to him just in time — he was almost dead."

"We've got to do something!" insisted Jane.

"We're getting him in AA, and he's promised he would go see a psychiatrist. We'll keep in touch with you," promised Diane.

Jane heard nothing more from Phoenix. She continued praying and hoping that Terry would be all right.

"But I still felt there was something wrong," states Jane, "and I couldn't put my finger on it. So on September 2, 1982, I took my sister-in-law out to see Armand. She had an appointment, and we went in a little early and talked with him. He said to me, "I **told** you the boy was suicidal. You've **got** to get him away from there. **Go get him! Don't wait — go get him!**""

A few days later Diane called again and told Jane that Terry was still drinking. He was staying at a buddy's house; this individual was also a heavy drinker. "Straight whiskey!" exclaimed Diane. "Terry's headed for self-destruction."

In the meantime, Jane had been discussing the developments with her son Chet, who was a police officer in Fontana. In spite of his skepticism about psychics, he made an appointment to see Armand personally on September 13, 1982.

Chet's last name is different from his mother's, since his father had died and Jane had remarried. According to Jane's account, Armand knew absolutely nothing about the mother-son relationship; in fact, he did not, typically, even ask Chet's name. Chet took along his mother's cassette recorder to give it another try.

"I have that tape," states Jane. "The recorder functioned perfectly. It's a half-hour session just like mine, and they discuss certain changes Armand thinks Chet's career is going to take."

But there was something else on the tape. "Armand told Chet he had a brother far away and that he was suicidal. He told him **he should go get him and bring him here**. And then he told Chet, 'After you bring him here, I want to see him and talk to him.' After I heard that tape, I **knew** we had to do something."

Chet had gone to Armand's on a Monday, Chet's day off. On

September 17 Jane took her friend Laura to the psychic's trailer for an appointment. They arrived a little early and Jane spoke to Armand briefly.

"I told him I didn't expect that he'd remember me, but reminded him what he'd told me about my son," recalls Jane. "He didn't seem to remember, but he sees so many people. I told him I'd recorded the session, but not one word had come out on the tape.

"He looked at me and said that that was an omen. That's all he said — he didn't explain. I didn't have any more time to ask what he meant."

Difficulty with tape recording equipment is not an uncommon occurrence among researchers of psychic phenomena. It is also reported frequently among investigators of UFO sightings, particularly those reports which seem to contain paranormal overtones. These are tape recorders which are in top condition, which function unfailingly on other occasions. This phenomenon is, in general, unexplainable at this point in time, although some researchers theorize that the jamming or failure to record represents psychokinetic interference from strong psychic sources.[5]

Armand was asked, in a later interview, about this phenomenon in Jane Robertson's case.

"A lot of times people will bring their tape recorders, and they won't work or something will go wrong," explained Armand. "I often feel it's an omen, indicating that if the tape were played back to someone who wasn't meant to hear it, it would hurt some other person. I remember when I told this woman that it was an omen. I meant there was a reason for this, and obviously she wasn't meant to tape it. She was supposed to act on the information, rather than play it back. If she'd taken a tape of the session back to other people and started playing it for them, they'd say, 'This guy's crazy! **You** know John — or her son, I don't know the name — **you** know how he is, **he** wouldn't do anything like that!'

"So, instead of playing the tape back to people who'd scoff and convince her not to do anything, she **acted** on the information that came through me. So in some cases, it's an omen. I wouldn't say in every case, however."

To continue, Jane's sister-in-law's session also recorded perfectly on Jane's recorder. Convinced by overwhelming evidence that she should act on Armand's warning, Jane and Chet drove to Phoenix on September 20, which was Chet's next day off. They went first to the home of Terry's parents-in-law, who told them that Terry was at the house owned by his drinking buddy, Bob. Chet, Jane and Diane went there together in the car. Jane had decided to let Chet handle the actual confrontation, for Terry had always respected Chet who, besides being an older brother, stood 6' 3" and weighed 250 pounds. He affectionately called him "the big moose."

They parked a little way down from Bob's house and Jane watched Chet approach the house. His knock was answered by Bob, and Jane observed the two men talking on the porch. She could hear their voices but could not distinguish the words. After a few minutes, Chet was ushered into the house.

"Diane and I sat in the car, talking," Jane relates. "Pretty soon Chet came out the door. He was carrying a small bag and Terry's shaving kit and he handed them to me through the window. He said, 'He's getting some of his stuff together, and he's going to go with us.' In fact, he told me **he** was going to come down to Chino tomorrow!"

Presently Terry came out the door and approached the car. What happened next, as described vividly by Jane Robertson, is inexplicable and chilling.

"Terry walked straight over to me," states Jane. "He leaned in the window of the car and squeezed me. Tears were running down his face and dropping onto mine. He's just not the type. I knew it was sheer desperation — it's something I can't explain. It was just like I was bringing him back from the dead.

"As he squeezed me, I felt like something was pulling hard inside me. I could feel it in every part of my body. I just felt — let me see if I can explain it."

To hear this strong, practical woman trying to describe an inexplicable occurrence gives one an eerie sensation, but what she says must be taken at face value, even though it cannot be explained in logical terms.

"Terry was holding me," restated Jane. "And it was **like there was a third body, or identity, there.** I just cannot put my finger on what it was. I felt like Armand was with us and had reached out and grabbed Terry. I can't say anymore than what I felt. It was something there. I don't know what it was.

"Then when Terry left me and walked around the front of the car and got in the back seat with Diane, I felt like something left my body. It was like — how would you say? Would it be a spirit? I felt like whatever it was in there pushing me to **go get him** was satisfied — that whatever it was felt fulfilled and the job was over."

Jane was questioned closely about this experience. At age thirty, she had had a near-death experience after being horribly injured in a motorcycle accident. She recounts how she felt herself leaving her body, seeing her own body lying in the street, watching her husband bending over her crying, and a doctor pronouncing her dead. But she cannot equate this apparent out-of-body experience with the sensation that occured in Phoenix.[16]

"I couldn't say whatever left was my spirit; I couldn't say it was part of Armand. But I felt a great pressure leaving, and then I could just **feel** that everything was going to be all right."

I asked if the feeling could have been just a normal sensation of vast relief. Jane answered definitely.

"No, no. It was something else, much stronger. It was so weird I can't even describe it. I've never felt anything like that in my life."

Terry bid a temporary goodbye to Diane and their children and accompanied his brother and mother on the drive back to Chino. He was silent for a long time and then gradually began to talk. Arriving home, Chet got him a temporary job at a nearby trucking firm as a dock worker, and Jane found him a little two-bedroom house and furnished it with odds and ends. Terry seemed happier than he had been for several years. He stopped drinking entirely, worked hard to pay the rent, and soon drove back to Phoenix to get his wife and children.

"One day he came over to pick up some dishes I'd got for them," recounts Jane in an October 19, 1982, interview. "I let him listen to Chet's tape. He said to me 'When you told me all this, mother, I can go along with **you** believing it, but I can't believe that the big moose believed it. But if **he** believed it, then I know it's got to be true.' "

Later, Terry told Chet that he planned to see Armand, as the psychic had requested. Armand does not know whether he ever did. What may have passed between them remains unknown, for besides the professional confidentiality Armand gives each client, the psychic has learned to blot out most of each day's readings from his conscious memory.

"If I didn't," he states simply, "I couldn't sleep."

"Believe me, when it comes to Armand," adds Jane Robertson, "I believe he's a miracle. Everything he told me on each of my children and their husbands and wives is so important to me. But most of all, I feel Armand snatched my son from Death's jaws!"

But what was the feeling of the "third identity" that joined Jane and Terry in their mother-son embrace? Even Armand cannot definitely explain it, although like the rest of us he can theorize. Perhaps his theory is the most logical of all.

"This lady had a magnetic force around her that brought her and me into strong contact," remembers Armand. "It was the contact, beginning an experience that we both had to go through. It seemed like it was a *karmic* contact — like probably in a past life I was some kind of minister that failed her, and in this life I had to make atonement for it by bringing back her son. I do not really know, for when I give these readings, I have to be very uninterested in myself. The whole thing here was to bring these two people together in a force of unity so they can go on with their lives.

"See, I'm just an intermediary for them. I don't **do** these things. God does them through me, and they follow through on His instruction. In other words, in order to bring about a unity between mother and son, I was the third party, as an intermediary. When she felt what she described as a third identity leaving, as soon as her son was safe again, she probably was remembering me, as the intermediary who'd brought them together.

"I sent her away with love and peace from that first session, and with certainty that what God had instructed would be accomplished. But peace couldn't reach her until she had actually found her lost son. The peace and harmony was finally reached by the contact of the two physical identities into the spiritual life. When she, holding the peace, touched him, he felt it, too; and he realized that he was still loved and wanted at home. The mother was the identity he needed to feel wisdom and strength of soul to be able to overcome his problems.

"So, really, three identities had brought about an action and a resultant tranquillity. When the two touched and felt it, the one — the intermediary — was no longer needed and it left, leaving two to work out their problems with the guidance of the Divine Light that was spread upon them."

Science may some day find a final answer to the puzzle. We await with interest.

These two cases, backed by affidavits from citizens who are not bound by legal restrictions can affirm that **prompt** use of a reliable psychic can predict the outcome in cases of missing persons as well as prevent tragedy in other situations. Use of psychics in puzzling murder cases and other violent felonies — before leads are lost and clues grow cold — could bring about a sharp upswing in crime solutions.

How long will it take before such use of psychics is common practice? How many tragedies could be prevented, and how many hours of agonized waiting prevented? Hopefully, we have demonstrated the values that can result if proper use of psychics is made at an appropriate time in the course of investigations. It is folly to use psychic assistance only as a last resort.

CHAPTER SEVEN

"Murders from the Past"

Murder is not a modern crime. Ever since Cain killed his brother Abel by beating him over the head with some heavy implement which he used to till the soil, the brutal compulsion to kill our brethren has surfaced instinctively from the darker recesses of the human mind.

The majority of murders are crimes of passion, of greed and of fear. They are, for the most part, not carefully planned, though we have had our "contract" murderers down through history plotted by, or directed toward, members of society from monarchs to Mafia.

Some persons who attempt to philosphize on the justice of life wonder how some people can go through life rather peacefully, neither killing nor being killed, while others are hapless victims of what seems to be an unequal Fate or, worse still, in the course of their lives, commit the crime of murder.

"It is not fair," one might say, "that I have had the advantages of a good family upbringing, a solid, love-filled marriage, children which grace my table and grow up to be fine strong adults, while others might be born and bred in slums, scrabble for food and clothing, and end up committing a senseless murder with a cheap gun while holding up a local shop proprietor for a few dollars."

Because the inequality of life is evident everywhere around us, many persons are beginning to suspect (if they have not already been convinced) that the idea of reincarnation, or successive lives, helps explain the apparent disparities in the lives of human beings.

Reincarnation **might be** an actual fact; it is stoutly accepted by most Hindus, who comprise about one-fifth of the world's population.

Among the members of other Eastern religions, and even in the Western world, where Christianity has not taught it — and indeed generally teaches against it — the notion of successive incarnations is gaining in popularity. Coupled with this, the notion of *karma*, both positive and negative, is gaining a handhold on the Western world. For the idea of *karma* — those deeds which, having been done by the individual in prior lives, either bring us rich rewards (positive) or demand payment of bad debts (negative) in our present existence — the idea of *karma* is so closely linked with the idea of reincarnation that the two theories cannot logically be separated. Without the idea of negative *karma*, in particular, successive lives would seem useless expenditure of time.[17]

Even the Catholic Church, from which the majority of the orthodox Christian Protestant religions have splintered, has no *ex cathedra* teaching against reincarnation. Generally accepted texts on Catholic dogma reject the idea, but some theologians feel that sincere Catholics can seek out the truth or untruth of reincarnation for themselves.

Many fundamentalist Christian churches abhor the idea, however, and for the sake of such readers it should be pointed out that the idea of successive lives is discussed here as a theory, not as an established fact. In perusing this chapter, such readers can openmindedly remember that the following case might be explained in ways other than by reincarnative function and negative *karmic* payment.

In prior chapters, and in pages yet to come, the notions of previous incarnations and *karmic* debt have been mentioned as they blend in naturally with each case discussed. This chapter, however, concerns a murder which occurred among Armand Marcotte's own circle of friends. Numerous details he recounts concerning it seem to indicate that the murder was closely linked karmically to that previous existence.

Armand first became acquainted with Raymond Llewelyn in 1975. At the time, the clairvoyant owned a large ranch in Fontana. There he raised Arabian horses — magnificent animals which not only provided financial remuneration from their sale but also helped satisfy his love of nature.

From time to time, the ranch hands whom Armand hired to take care of the horses and other chores would quit their jobs, leaving the ranch shorthanded. Most of them were rovers who worked a few weeks or months and then, with money in their jeans, would pack their belongings and move on.

One day a client who regularly patronized Armand's "Hair Safari" in Upland mentioned that she knew of a runaway kid who needed a job. The boy had papers showing he was eighteen and legally able to be on his own. This patron worked for a local social service organization, and described the young man to Armand as bright and willing to work, but unable to find a suitable job and lodging. Knowing that Armand often hired temporary hands on his ranch, she told him about this young fellow.

Armand didn't happen to need any more ranch workers at that time, but he had, and still has, a soft spot in his heart for strays.

"Raymond came and applied for a job, but I didn't have any job," recalls Armand. "I had a bunkhouse where he could sleep and where there would be food if he needed it . So I interviewed him first and then offered a temporary job to him until he could get on his feet. The bunkhouse was off the barn, but it had cots where the ranch hands stayed."

So another stray became a hand, caring for Armand's Arabian horses. But this young man, Raymond Llewelyn, was different from the others who stayed awhile and then moved on. For Raymond stayed.

"He worked for me," says Armand, with an atypical sadness in his eyes. "You know, I sort of took a shine to him. There was a fondness about him, too, and a magic type of situation developed. He stayed on and on. Eventually, he got other jobs around town, but he stayed on with me.

"Raymond was a very strong, meticulous person. He was a Virgo, and they like everything to be orderly — always picking things up and putting them away. But another thing about him, he had Capricorn rising, and I'm Capricorn.

"A sort of father-son relationship developed between us. Raymond had been an orphan, and he was adopted when he was seven or eight. But he didn't get along well with his adoptive mother and father, and they had a lot of problems with him. Eventually it got so bad in his later teens that he ran away from his home in Connecticut, making his way out to California.

"He kept asking me to adopt him," reminisces Armand. "He used to sign his name 'Raymond Marcotte' — and I kept saying, 'There's no need for me to adopt you. You've got your parents.' "

Raymond stayed on, signing his name "Raymond Marcotte" whenever it pleased him to do so, in spite of Armand's kindly objections. In 1978 Armand sold his ranch to a subdivider, and watched a new community of houses fill the land where once the Arabian horses grazed. A trailer court was built on the eastern edge of the land, and here the psychic kept a small trailer for use when he was in town.

He moved to Hesperia, purchasing a large mobile home in an

attractive section of that desert town. By this time, Raymond was like part of the family and had his own room in the new residence.

Always a good-looking youth, his features were set off by thick, black curly hair. The only thing which marred his appearance in any way was an unexplained streak of pure white hair which grew out in the back of his head. Raymond knew only that this pencil-sized strand was probably growing from a site of a birthmark. He'd had it as long as he could remember.

The young man no longer worked with the Arabian horses, for they had been sold along with the ranch. But he continued working at other jobs and eventually was hired at Big Boy's restaurant as a trainee for a management position. For a young man of twenty-one years, he was coming up in the world. He had everything to live for.

He purchased a car and was making payments on a small mobile home of his own, which he rented out for additional income.

In the meanwhile, Armand had started teaching informal classes on psychic development techniques in his Hesperia home. The classes were open to anyone who was interested. Teaching came naturally to Armand — he enjoyed the interaction among the group members, watching their psychic talents grow, experimenting on new methods of research and delving into little understood branches of metaphysics.

One evening in 1978, at the weekly class, one of the students brought a book on reincarnation. It suggested that former lives, lost in memory, might be relived through hypnotic regression.[18]

Raymond never really joined the classes wholeheartedly, since his mind was on more practical things — like his current girl friend and making money. This evening, however, Armand and the group teased Raymond into being a hypnotic subject. No one in the group was an expert, but with the aid of a book on hypnotic techniques, Raymond was hypnotically regressed.

He lay down on the couch, and with the guidance of an amateur hypnotist, became totally relaxed. After a countdown from ten to one, he was told,

"You're a baby. What are you doing?"

Raymond obligingly made sounds and actions like a baby lying in its crib.

"You're going back beyond this life," Raymond was told, as the instructions in the book were followed for regressing to "past lives." Slowly, he was brought to what might have been another consciousness back in an unknown time.

"Where are you?" he was asked.

"I'm on a sugar plantation," Raymond stated.

"Where?"

"I don't know... tropical. I can't tell because I can't read. I'm colored."

Raymond was Caucasian, but was ostensibly dredging up memories of a life in which he had been partly black — what was formerly called a light-skinned "mulatto."

"Everyone thinks I'm handsome," volunteered Raymond in the hypnotic state. "Oh! I'm flirting with the mistress of the plantation. She has a fourteen-year-old daughter I'm in love with, and I'm trying to get to the daughter through her mother. She won't let me near her daughter otherwise."

Further inquiries into this intriguing situation brought forth information from Raymond that he was thirty-two years old and a worker on the plantation. He lived in a tent-like shack on the grounds. His handsome appearance had caught the roving eye of the plantation owner's wife, a woman about fifty years old.

Raymond, as he explained, did not really like the woman. She was too old to attract him, but the sweet innocence of her beautiful daughter captured his greed. He pretended to love the mother, returning numerous times to her bedroom in the late hours of the night.

Finally, he convinced the young girl to visit him in his shack, where they consummated his passion. Several times she came until one night the mother, suspecting something, followed her daughter.

Startled, Armand's metaphysics class listened as Raymond relived the details of his dilemma with full emotion.

"Oh, my God! The mother catches us together! She's **furious** because her daughter is after me. The mother considers me **her** lover. She threatens me that she'll have me killed if we see each other again. But the mother is at least fifteen or twenty years older than I am. I want the daughter!

"But the mother is so much in love with me she doesn't want to turn me in," continued Raymond, in turmoil. "But she tells me if she catches us again she'll have me shot! She doesn't want her husband to find out. He's the landowner, and his word is law!"

Still in hypnotic state, Raymond described how the secret visits continued. He'd meet the girl in different places, meanwhile keeping trysts with the mother so she would not suspect anything. But woman's intuition being what it is, the mother was not satisfied that Raymond was being "faithful" to her.

She pretended one day to make a trip into the city, Port-au-Prince, and let it be known that she would not be back until the next morning. Raymond and his young paramour took advantage of the situation and stayed together that night in the girl's bedroom.

Meanwhile, the mother returned home in the middle of the night and stormed into her daughter's room. She had a gun and advised Raymond to stand still or she would shoot him. She screamed to the plantation guard nearby, demanding that he shoot the young traitor.

As the guard rushed in, his gun drawn, Raymond wrenched the gun from the mother's grip. As the guard raised his gun to fulfill his mistress's orders, Raymond shot the young girl in the stomach, killing her almost immediately. He shouted, "If I can't have her, **nobody will!**"

He, himself, died as the guard fired into the back of his head. As he died, Raymond could hear the guard boasting, "It's just like shooting a coconut off the shelf!"

"The guard said this because the young man — Raymond — was black, and the policeman was white," explains Armand. "So he fell, and died, and the girl died, and in the death there was darkness where they couldn't find one another in the spirit life, because one had brought on the death of the other, and the girl was paying the price of her immoral love affair. And Raymond kept saying, while he was still hypnotized, that he could hear the mother screaming in anguish over the death of her daughter. She hadn't meant it to go that far, but the act had been committed and there was no way to bring her daughter back."

Raymond, meanwhile, was trying to wake up from the hypnotic state. He was feeling the pain associated with his "death," and the class members brought him back with some difficulty. After he regained total consciousness, he had no memory of the life and death he had appeared to relive.

"We told him what he had said," states Armand, "and he thought that was ridiculous."

That ended the experiments with regression, at least for the time being. The event had been too much of a traumatic surprise for all concerned — except Raymond, who remembered nothing.

The event, however, started Armand thinking. Partly through intuition and partly through logic, he became convinced that the snow-white streak in Raymond's mass of curly, coal-black hair marked the spot where a bullet had entered and killed in that prior life. Armand considered the situation in the light of the *karmic*-debt theory and decided to warn his young friend.

"I said to him, 'Raymond, you're going to have to be careful. If you don't do God's work in this life, he'll take you out of the picture very early because you caused a death.'

"He said to me, 'According to you, I **died** for it. That paid off my debt to society.' 'I told him, 'Raymond, that isn't right, because in God's eyes, justice has to be made, and in **your** case, you're going to have to die young in order to know what it's like to take that life in its prime. Because this girl had everything to live for, and you took her life. Although you paid for it, you still have to know what it's like to die early. So you better start following the Golden Rule, or else you'll find yourself at an early death.' Raymond wasn't really a bad kid, but he'd gotten lots of speeding tickets that he tried to hide from me, and other things like that.

"And that's all that was said. Meanwhile, right after the New Year of 1979, my class was getting ready to graduate, and so, to test their psychic abilities, I decided to have them all 'read' Raymond independently. We would compare the results later to see whether or not they matched.

"You see, I'd had a vision about Raymond," Armand explains. "Early in the New Year, I concentrated on Raymond and I kept hearing a woman screaming. I told him about this and told him it was like the scream **he** had heard after he shot the girl in his prior life.

"Raymond was planning to go up to Muscle Beach with a beautiful young girl and another young man. All three of them worked the night shift at Big Boy's restaurant. Raymond and the other boy were both interested in this girl and vied for her attention, all in a friendly, competitive way. They planned to leave early, about 4:00 AM after their shift ended, drive up the coast, spend the day, and be home late that night.

"But I could see violent danger around him if he took that trip. Partly to confirm my own impressions and partly to test my students, we all read him on the Wednesday before he planned the trip. It was January 10, 1979.

"They all told him their psychic impressions about what was going on in his life. My students read first, of course, because I didn't want my impressions to influence them so they'd be reading my mind, or something.

"Well, they all told him not to take the trip he was planning on Saturday. Raymond would not listen to the group's advice. He had never accepted their story about what he had said while he was hypnotized. Even when I told him that there would be a tragedy if he went ahead with his plans, Raymond scoffed at the warning.

"The day before the trip, Raymond walked into his bank and

borrowed $2,500 on his own. For twenty-two years of age, this was quite an accomplishment. He had acquired some bills on his mobile home and needed the extra money to make repairs. He liked his job and was on the way to becoming a manager at the restaurant.

Above all, he looked forward to a marvelous time at the beach the following day. Armand's warning impressed him not at all — neither did the confirmations offered by the metaphysics students.

Early in the morning of January 13, 1979, Raymond and his two friends started off. They stopped in Hollywood at a restaurant near the Hollywood Theatre. After a leisurely breakfast, they came out of the restaurant, walking toward Raymond's car. There was a crowd of about twenty people on the sidewalk in front of the theater, waiting for a bus.

A young black security guard, gun on hip, was among them, on his way home from his work nearby.

"The guard walks by and starts making passes at the girl, getting fresh," recounts Armand. "Raymond tried to make him apologize. They argued, a struggle developed, and the guard pulled the gun on Raymond and **shot** him — in the stomach!

"Two policemen saw it," he continued. "They ran up and arrested the fellow, and Raymond lay dying in the arms of his friend and the young girl kept screaming — the identical scream I'd heard in my vision, like the scream Raymond described as the mother's when her daughter was shot.

"And Raymond died," Armand concluded, his voice grating with remembered sorrow. "He had everything to live for, just like that young girl in his prior life. And Raymond found out what it was like to die young, when everything was going great guns for him."

Early that Saturday morning, at the moment of Raymond's death, Armand woke up screaming, "They've killed Raymond!" He had no logical knowledge of the tragedy, yet he instinctively knew something was very wrong. It was Saturday, but his cosmetology studio was open for business as usual. Saturday was one of their busiest days.

Thrusting his fears deep into his subconscious, Armand decided not to believe that anything had happened to Raymond. He forced himself to believe that his young friend was all right and would come home as usual that evening, safe and happy. For in spite of his visions and intuitive impressions, Armand was not, at that time, always confident of his own abilities. He often had doubts, especially on impressions where he did not receive immediate, positive feedback.

"I went to work, and I tried to be happy," states Armand. "I put it out of my mind because I didn't want to have anything to do with

creating a tragedy, if such a thing were possible. Raymond had said to me, 'Don't worry — I'll be home.' I didn't want even to think about it.

"But he wasn't coming home. When I got home myself that afternoon, I found a note on my door to call the police in Hollywood. I didn't do it. And the police called me again.

"As Raymond was dying, he told them to call me, that I was his next of kin. He told them I was his father, and he said to the policemen who were there, 'Call Armand and tell him I love him.' And he died."

When the Hollywood policeman called Armand again, he was told that Raymond had been shot, that they had rushed him to a hospital, but that he had died on the way. He told the police he had been adopted by Armand.

"He had died when the moon was full," explains Armand. "That night he appeared to me. I'd been crying all evening, since I'd learned. He said, 'I'm dead, ain't I?' And I said, 'Yes.' "

Raymond appeared in visible form, like a mosaic painting, clusters of color coming together to form the shape so familiar in life. He was dressed casually, as he ordinarily dressed — no white robe or brilliant halo for this troubled spirit.

"Oh, Raymond! Why did you go? I **warned** you," Armand remembers saying.

"I don't want to die! I don't **want** to be dead!" lamented Raymond.

"It's already too late. You're dead," explained Armand. "Go toward the light. Go towards the light. I'll pray for you." And Raymond's form disappeared.

Armand made the tragic drive to Hollywood to claim Raymond's body, but being unable to present proof of next of kin, he was denied permission. Raymond's body lay in the county morgue for ten days while Armand attempted to work out arrangements with the boy's adoptive parents.

During this difficult period, Armand kept thinking about the impressions he'd been receiving over the past months — perceptive hints that Raymond would be going away.

"I kept saying to him, 'Raymond, you're going to be leaving me. I don't know where you're going, but I won't see you for a long, long time.' And he kept saying, 'You're crazy. I'll be there. Don't worry, I'm **not** leaving. I'm happy here. I've got everything. Why would I leave you? I want you to be my father, and you won't adopt me,' and this sort of thing. You see, **he** knew something, subconsciously, that I didn't fully see then, and that was that he was coming toward his death. He kept saying how he hated his adoptive parents, and he didn't want to be around them. He didn't even want to be buried with them.

"We even talked about things like that. He told me if he died he wanted to be cremated. We had talked about this the week before, because I wanted him to make a will. I even thought I was going to die, because I was beginning to see a death around us."

Armand had never pressed for details of why Raymond so disliked his parents. But now, with the young man dead, and unable to claim the body, Armand called Raymond's parents. They received the news stonily. "So he got what was coming to him," commented his father, and told Armand they would make arrangements with the Hollywood police to have him shipped home to Connecticut.

Armand, however, recalled what Raymond had said about not wanting to be buried in Connecticut, in the event of his death. The clairvoyant suggested to the man that if they would release the body in his care, he would give it the funeral Raymond had said he wanted. He also offered to take care of all the expenses.

Raymond's parents' response was to ask Armand to put his offer in writing! He sent them a telegram accepting all responsibilities and fees. The parents, in turn, sent a telegram to the authorities releasing the body to Armand.

All this took ten days. At the end of the long wait Armand arranged a memorial service at a Covina, California, crematorium and invited all of Raymond's friends to attend a memorial service. Nobody came. Armand was the only one there to bid farewell.

"It just broke me down, being the only one, and then I went home," recalls Armand. "But he appeared to me again on the night of the next full moon, February 11. He said, 'It's just like you said it was, Armand. I found my mother and some of my real relatives. It's just like you said it would be in the spirit world. I've paid my debt.' "

"His karmic debt had been paid," states Armand. "And now he was studying to do things later on. He was a **whiz** in electronics. He could do anything with electricity, the telephone — he could fix **anything**. He said, 'I'm adjusting to it here, and I'll see you one more time.' And then he disappeared."[19]

The details around the tragic death seemed, in Armand's opinion, to fit into Raymond's supposed earlier death in a prior incarnation. According to what Armand has been able to perceive, the mother in the earlier life was the girl whom Raymond and his buddy both admired. It was she who screamed as Raymond lay dying on the pavement. And an additional explanation for the white streak in the back of Raymond's head of black hair was perceived by the clairvoyant. Not only could it be the point at which the bullet had entered Raymond's head in that former life, but the whiteness of the streak of hair resembled **juice pouring out of a coconut**. Was this the final *karmic* symbol? Or a synchronistic puzzle? The guard who had shot Raymond in the former life had laughed as he said, "It's just like shooting coconuts off a shelf!"

For the third month, at the time of the full moon, March 13, 1979, Raymond appeared again, in now-familiar clusters of colored light forming into mosaics, then coming together to give Raymond's spirit visible form. This time he told Armand that he would not see him for a long time, and that he would be there to greet him when Armand himself would "cross over." After that visit, the psychic thought no more about it. He continued to pray and have Masses said for Raymond's soul; his deep grief spent itself and finally left. Raymond was released and in his heaven.

For some reason unknown to Armand, the boy's death seemed to give a push to the clairvoyant's psychic work. He became more involved in research, experimenting with his psychic abilities, and developing his talents further.

"Then on Thanksgiving Day, it's like he came back to thank me. I was sitting reading a book, and this bright light filled the room. I didn't look up from my book, but apparently the light was the mosaic forming again into Raymond's spirit-form. I heard my little dog whimper, and I looked up and there Raymond was. He was smiling — that's all he was doing.

"I remembered he'd told me he wouldn't see me again until I crossed over, and I knew I wasn't dying. I couldn't figure it out. I thought, 'Show me a sign I'm not asleep or dreaming.' "

When questioned about this reaction, Armand explained that he had been told by the holy men in India that he "would do something for mankind." He figured he hadn't done it yet. He was still studying and **reading**. When Raymond paid the extra visit, Armand did not feel ready to cross over because he had not yet set in motion the thing, whatever it was, that he was supposed to do.

"Raymond used to brush my little dog all the time whenever he came home from work, and she'd always run over and get her brush for him when she'd see him come into the room. Well, this day, Thanksgiving 1979, my little dog ran over and got her hairbrush which was in the bathroom and brought it and put it at Raymond's feet, where he was standing. Then I knew I wasn't dreaming. He smiled and went off in peace, and I haven't dreamed or seen him in visions since."

The story of Raymond is more than a touching saga of a young stray who was taken in by a kindly mentor. The fact that Armand felt his own psychic faculties increase and his own confidence in his abilities drastically increase suggests that Raymond, in the spirit world, might have somehow been a catalyst for this phenomenon. We cannot know for sure, of course, until, as Armand states Raymond said, "I'll be there to greet you when you cross over."

Since Raymond's death particularly, Armand's desire to teach others has doubled and redoubled. We can theorize that, besides paying his negative *karmic* debt through his tragic death, Raymond fulfilled a positive *karmic* debt, perhaps one owed to Armand himself by Raymond from a still earlier life.

CHAPTER EIGHT

"...and Lost Bodies from the Deeper Past"

Wednesday, June 16, 1981, dawned cool in Los Angeles. The damp marine layer typical of that month clung around my Pasadena home. In Brea, where Dr. Dorothea Kenny was getting ready to make the forty-five-mile trip to Fontana, it was somewhat warmer, for Orange County cities are typically more sheltered from the ocean's blanket of moist air.

The fifty-mile freeway drive from Pasadena to Fontana was unfamiliar to me. "Fontana" had always been just a name on a map, a semi-desert community where the Kaiser steel mills were situated. I had never before met anyone who lived there.

Thea, her short brown curls topping her diminutive but determined form, made her way northeast as I traveled east, for we had decided it would be easier to meet in Fontana to keep our appointment with Armand Marcotte. Beside me on the car seat were my briefcase, tape recorder, maps, files — and a small white-and-blue box, the innocuous appearance of which gave no hint of its contents — an object of intense interest.

I had been introduced to Louise Ludwig and the PsiCom group by Thea Kenny. Thea, a native of Ireland transplanted in America, had earned her Ph.D. in Indo-European archeology and mythology, and was a professor at a state university. Irish, with an archeology background, she was deeply interested in what had become known as my "Irish project."

The object in the white-and-blue box had already been psychometrized by PsiCom. At that time, however, it had been wrapped in paper toweling, deposited inside a glass jelly jar and taken to

PsiCom by Thea at my request. They "read" the object through the sealed jar. At the end of the fascinating readings, Thea gave the members minimal feedback. The object, she told them, was a scrap of bone relevant to an Irish psychic archeology project.

My Irish project involved history, mystery, romance, drama and death; the bone-scrap was laden with emotional content. After PsiCom had conducted a second psychometric session with the bone, at which I was present (for at that point it didn't matter whether the members might be reading my mind), Dr. Ludwig had suggested we might try asking Armand Marcotte to help us. We had never heard the name, but she assured us he was a very good clairvoyant and would probably donate his services for a scientific project. That was good news; my research funds were low.

Thea made the appointment with Armand by phone, informing him only that she had been referred by Dr. Ludwig and that the reading concerned a project of scientific importance.

So events were set in motion for my first meeting with Armand. Nearing Fontana, I felt the air become hot, dusty and still. Smoke from the steel mills blurred the blue desert sky. Twice I passed the location where Armand had his trailer, for the entrance was camouflaged with bottlebrush bushes.

Entering along the unpaved driveway, I saw Trailer #9, perched next to an empty swimming pool. A small weathered brown-and-yellow sign read, "Armand Marcotte."

Thea's blue Datsun was parked nearby. As we knocked on Armand's trailer door, neither of us knew what to expect, for Louise had told us as little about him as Thea had told him about the project at hand — nothing. When he invited us in there were few preliminaries, and little chitchat; he was eager to start on this "project of scientific importance" which his friend Dr. Ludwig had referred to him.

I laid the small box in front of him and asked him to give his impressions about the object inside. He grinned good naturedly and began to concentrate.

"I get a religious thing — it once belonged to a religious person. The person who had this thing was on to something. And it was either taken away from him or stolen from him. This seemed to be a clue that people left behind," he began.

So far, Armand seemed to be batting a thousand.

"It's made out of wood?" he asked. "And lead, is it?"

"Well, lead and wood are associated with it," said Thea.. The main bone from which the object in the box had been derived had been found by my team in 1978, nearly tucked away, between a stone ledge and a pile of lead-lined, wood-covered coffins in an ancient burial vault in Dublin, Ireland.

"It has carving or something on it, like a scratch," Armand continued. This was true. Most of the bone-scrap had been carved into splinters and converted into collagen for Carbon-14 dating. Only a scrap had been retained for use as a psychometric object. The main part from which the bone had been taken was the major portion of a human cranium, and this had been left in the care of Irish officials.

"It appears somebody stepped on it or ran over it, or something like that," continued Armand, his brow wrinkling in concentration. "It was overlooked for a while before it was found. I keep getting this is a very serious situation. The person who owned this is dead."

All direct hits, from a clairvoyant who knew nothing about what the object in the box could possibly be, except that he was able to pull information out of the Cosmic Mind. The burial vault where the cranium had been found had been disused since 1868. It contained twelve bodies — members of the Irish family of the Earls of Meath. The cranium had not come from any of the coffins in the vault, for they were all essentially intact. It had belonged to another skull, identity unknown. My investigative team, eleven months before, had painstakingly sifted the loose soil on the vault floor and had discovered a few small bits of the skull. We had surmised they had been broken off and scattered by the boots of long-dead Irish laborers who had borne the Meath coffins to their resting-place.

"There seems to be another part to it, and they need this part to make a picture, and it appears to be a design of some kind that will lead to something," continued the clairvoyant.

Armand **was,** as Louise had assured us, a very good psychic. For our team's main purpose in searching the earthen floor of the vault was to recover all the missing parts of the ancient cranium and all the facial bones, most especially the jaw. The search which I had started in 1977, and on which I had spent thousands in personal funds, was for the purpose of finding, and reconstructing, the skull of the Irish patriot, Robert Emmet.

It was an Irish mystery of the first order — not only the location of Emmet's severed head but also the resting place of his headless body. The young patriot had been executed for high treason against the English crown in 1803. His head had been cut off and lost, and his headless body had been buried in an unknown grave. It was important for the Irish to find Robert's grave, for in a stirring speech on the eve of his death he had uttered these immortal words:

> "Let no man write my epitaph. Let my memory remain in
> oblivion and my tomb remain uninscribed...When my
> country takes her place among the nations of the earth,
> then, and not till then, let my epitaph be written."[20]

Robert Emmet had lived on in Irish history, poetry and song. His valorous spirit had inspired other patriots to fight and die, and fight and win until twenty-six counties of Ireland had attained the status of an independent republic. The synchronistic yearning of the Irish to find their hero's grave had to be satisfied. I, an American of Irish descent, had entered the search, using the method of psychic archeology.

Armand was a link in a long chain of psychics who had psychometrized the cranial bone, trying to determine if it was, indeed, part of Emmet's skull. Since Armand was experienced in helping solve modern murders and missing-person cases, it was logical to think that he might help solve a case of a missing body from the historical past.

Now, still without seeing what was in the box and having no knowledge about the project, Armand pencil-sketched the unseen object. He made a representational drawing, very similar to the actual shape.

"The person who died — it wasn't a natural death. He went into a type of convulsion before he was done in." Then his natural curiosity took over. "Let me feel the object. Have I identified it for you?"

"Could you give us an impression of the personality of the person who was associated with that object?" I asked.

"I'll have to touch it because I wouldn't be able to do it — " He opened the box. "Oh, yeah," he remarked, delighted that he'd sketched it accurately. He began to feel the bone-scrap, concentrating anew.

"I also get that the man who killed this man wore a robe, could be a religious robe. I keep getting vivid colors, golds and reds. This man wasn't very old, couldn't have been over thirty-two. An older man, in his forties or fifties, killed him. This man was not married. I see a relationship with the older man, a triangle situation. This is a jealousy-type of crime, an intimate type situation. The two of them probably had an affair."

My inner antennae sprang alert. Armand seemed to be saying that the man of the bone had probably had a homosexual relationship with his killer. This could not be Robert Emmet, whose pure idealism and virtue had been recognized even by his enemies, and who had been described by his friend Thomas Moore, the famous Irish poet and lyricist, as "wholly free from the follies and frailties of youth."

Either Armand was mistaken, or the man of the bone was **not** Robert Emmet, but another unfortunate who had also been decapitated centuries ago.

My investigative team had found the cranium in St. Catherine's Church vault in 1978.[21] We had been led directly to it by a reading given by a well-known clairvoyant from Washington State, a man who had a good record in the growing field of psychic archeology. Many psychics had worked on the find before we contacted Armand, but their impressions had proved a puzzling mixture. A lot of the perceptual material fitted a man **like** Emmet, but some of the material **did not** fit. Now, here Armand was telling us that the man of the bone had been secretly murdered by another, with whom his relationship had been, at best, unsavory.

"There's a man still living who knows the story," continued Armand. "He has trouble with one arm. It's partly crippled, the right arm. He's had a stroke."

"Perhaps you're getting something we know nothing about," I suggested, shutting off feelings of inner dismay.

"Well," added Thea, pointedly. "This is definitely a person we know nothing about, unless we ourselves are on the wrong track."

"I think you're on the wrong track, that's what I get," agreed Armand.

Without sharing any details concerning the project, we asked him to describe how and where the bone had been found. He said it was next to a shed or barn, perhaps where fruit and vegetables were kept; at the time of the death this building was not in a residential area but stood among open, green fields. The place where the man had been buried, however, was dark and enclosed.

"Dark and enclosed," indeed. When we first entered the basement vault, it had been sealed for ten years and untouched for over seventy-five. The yellow glow of our Tilley lamp had barely cut through the pitch blackness. It was with utter surprise, back in July 1978, that we had seen the coffins, lying in heaps and piles, the older ones crumpled under the weight of the ones on top, giving the effect of a graveyard in upheaval.

St. Catherine's Church had been inside the city of Dublin in 1803, the date of Emmet's death. Was Armand seeing back to an earlier time — perhaps as far back as four hundred years ago — when Dublin had not yet encroached on the green fields and vineyards belonging to the monks who, at that time, owned this church? For, although I had not yet received the final results of the carbon-dating tests, examination of the cranium by Irish scientists had established that the bones were probably 200 to 400 years old.

"The man threatened to expose the older one." Armand's impressions were coming fast. "They were probably both in a religious sect. The older man got another man to help him bury the body. This man waited until the older man died, too, and then he wrote what happened in a letter and hid it in the record books which were kept on shelves in this place."

I was grateful the tape cassette was recording it all; Armand's impressions were coming fast.

"The man with a crippled arm found the letter telling about it. I keep getting a wall of books. He has kept the letter because he didn't want to degrade these people who lived before him."

By this time Armand had correctly identified the location as Ireland. Thea's soft accent might have given a clue to this, but in view of the correct material he was perceiving it was more likely that he had received that information, also, by psychometric means.

"Look in the library," advised Armand. "The man who found this letter didn't know what to do about it, and the people in charge of the place decided it should be kept quiet. Because the people are still there — it's still a religious group."

"Where is the rest of this man's body?" I asked.

"He buried him in two different places. There was a wagon involved, and I'm sure you should have found some of his collar bone. See? This is what you should have found." And Armand thumped his own clavicle where it joined near a shoulder.

I realized abruptly something I had almost forgotten. In digging for the jawbone, I had uncovered a mass roughly equal to the shape and size of a jawbone, directly underneath where the cranium had been found on the surface. I recalled how the Irish dental surgeon, Dr. Barry, had urged me on in uncovering this, for we both felt it might be a long-buried jawbone belonging to the cranium. But instead of a jawbone, the mass had turned out to be the outer part of a clavicle, belonging to a shallowly buried, intact skeleton, interred without a coffin only four inches under the earth in the vault floor.

"Do you know the neck spine? Did you find any of these vertebrae?" asked Armand, indicating the back of his own neck.

We had, indeed, found two vertebrae while sifting the surface soil and they, too, were in the care of Irish officials. One had been split, as by a sharp blow. Its finding had excited us, for it possibly meant that it had come from a head which had been severed from the body, as was Emmet's, by an executioner's knife.

I didn't say anything like this to Armand. "We found what seemed to be two vertebrae," I offered.

"Now the other part of the body — you should find the other part — there should be another building, with stone front, in front of it. Like it could have been a coal cellar or like, where they put fruit in a cellar. I would say it would be buried back in back of an entrance, in front of a wall, because at that time they were building that addition. Is there a stone wall there that's part of that building?"

"Of the same building? "Of the dark enclosed place?" I inquired.

"Yes!" said Armand.

I thought about how the 1978 exploration had revealed that part of the cellar basement contained an antique floor heating system, dating back to the 1700s. This had been added long after the church had been built. Could this be linked to the "coal cellar" and "addition" Armand had mentioned? I answered that the basement area was segmented by numerous stone walls.

"Well, this stone wall's by the foundation. They built a wall in front of where the rest of the body is buried."

I was getting confused and must have shown it. Armand snatched up a piece of paper and began to draw a rough map.

"This bone should have been right about **here**, in a corner, like. OK. There should be an alcove under the ground. You don't see it on top, but underground, but they put a wall in front of it. This bone you have here was in the corner more. You'll find a hollow place in back there somewhere, and there would be part of the body in that area. Because the wall was built **in front** of that where it was buried. It was done like, ten or fifteen years later."

"So this bone could have gotten separated from the rest accidentally?" asked Thea.

"That's right," Armand nodded. "Because when they built this wall, they dug the foundation. In digging, they were throwing the dirt toward the corner."

"In what area would we find this alcove?" I asked. Armand might be a brilliant psychic but his drawing ability was not da Vinci.

"It's like a wine cellar, or a fruit cellar, all underground," he replied.

"So the body was all buried together to begin with?" asked Thea.

"Yeah," Armand agreed. "And that's why you should have picked up a couple of vertebrae. And the rest of it is under in here. Like it was laid out this way, the body, see?" He drew more on the map. "And the head and things were here, where they put the footing for the wall. They dug this out and shoved the head over **there** in the corner and built the wall where the head **used to be**."

He drew more, indicating the position where the cranium of the murdered man had first lain when buried, then indicated the corner of the alcove where the head was thrown together with a couple of neck vertebrae after it was accidentally severed from the rest of the skeleton, by the sharp shovels of the laborers who dug the foundation for the wall.

I stared at the sketch. It bore an amazing resemblance, rough though it was, in proportion and shape, to a sketch I had carefully prepared for the Irish officials and members of the research team, after our 1981 retrieval of the cranium from St. Catherine's basement. Ten of the Meath caskets were piled **in an alcove** separated from the rest of a segmented basement room by a two-and-one-half-foot-high wall. The cranium which we had hoped could be verified as Emmet's had been found near the corner of the alcove, tucked between the end of a bottom casket and the dividing wall. And right alongside this pile of caskets, we had accidentally discovered the uncoffined skeleton four inches below the surface. We had uncovered not only the clavicle, but part of one side of the rib cage and one hand and arm. I had taken a couple of finger bones, thinking that they would provide a good control experiment to compare with the carbon-dating on the cranium.

The skeleton beneath the surface was not associated with the Meath burials. I had given my word none of these caskets would be disturbed. The buried, uncoffined skeleton lay about eight inches out of line with the Meath coffins, and its skull was out of view entirely, being at least one foot ahead of the front end of the Meath caskets. In other words, **the jawbone and other missing head bones of the buried skeleton evidently still lay under the wall which separated the Meath alcove from the rest of the basement room.**

My confidence in Armand's ability returned. There was no way he could have known about the buried skeleton. The only feedback Thea and I had given him up to that point was that a stray cranium and a couple of vertebrae had been found.

I listened with an open mind as he described the murdered man.

"He was going to expose the older man. This young man had been draining the older man of finances. The man had a lot of pressure on his chest during the death process. He couldn't breathe, his lungs were giving him trouble. But I think the final blow was to the head — and his eyes — **oh!** He's having trouble with his eyes. His right eye — it's hurting like you wouldn't believe! He can't see out of one eye!"

Was this another direct hit? While sifting the loose soil in the vault near where the cranium was found, we had uncovered a round bone which Dr. Barry had identified as an eye socket, probably belonging to the cranium in question.

"This young man could be very cruel," continued Armand. "He had a mean streak. His mouth was very dry before he died because they've cut off water or liquids from him for a while.

"When the man that killed this man died, an account of the murder was written by the man who helped the murderer bury the body. I keep getting it put into a book, and it was discovered and it's still around. It's in a very old manuscript like a record book. Are there any record books around that place?"

"There should be," I answered. "I haven't located them, but there should be."

"Well, there are record books, and it tells exactly what was going on. The young man didn't always stay there. He'd stay for about three months, and then he'd go off again. But he kept coming back to the older man. And the young man had nobility around him, not that **he** was from royalty, but he associated with people in high places."

"Do you get a name for the older man, or any identifying information?" I asked.

"I get a W," Armand answered. "Like Wilbur or Wilbert... and I get a G, like Gancy or Gansey or something. But I feel that his death was documented, in a letter, and it's going to be found.

"If you search the period of the year this young man died, it would be in that record book... I see a 6 or a 9, and I get it on the shelves. It could be Volume 9 or 6, because I can't tell if it's up or down. If they're not **in** this building, they're close to it. A school... or a college. I see a big wall, and these old books that were in this building at one time. Like an archive, where there are historical things. I see people walking by, looking, like it's a collector's item or something. And the letter was found by a man living today, who has a paralyzed arm, and he kept quiet about it, like I said."

Returning home from the session, I transcribed the tape cassette and studied Armand's map. Could he be right? Were we on the wrong track, as the clairvoyant had stated so definitely early in the reading? Was the stray cranium I hoped could be identified as Emmet's merely discarded remains of a secretly murdered man?

Several weeks later, the final Carbon-14 dating results were obtained. The lab had dated not only collagen from the cranium but collagen extracted from the finger bones of the buried skeleton. **The dates of each** were surprisingly similar.

Although the results were clothed in technical language, the upshot of the analysis was that both dated from the mid-1500s. It was very possible that the cranium and finger bones belonged to the same individual, as Armand had stated.

Realizing how accurate Armand's reading had been, I set about trying to verify the other parts — namely, that an account of the murder had been written down and that the manuscript existed to this day.

Many church records dating from the time of the Reformation, especially in Ireland, had been destroyed by persons caught up in the violence of the time. But ancient manuscripts from St. Catherine's Church and the monks in charge of that parish at the time in question do exist. Correspondence with Dublin archivists had not yet revealed the existence of the "letter" described by Armand, but my search continues. This has nothing to do, anymore, with the Emmet project but is an interesting spinoff from it.

The carbon-dating results had proven that the cranium, first thought to be that of Robert Emmet, was not his. I continued the search, using the multiple-psychic method. The problem of locating the grave of Emmet had become rather hopelessly entangled, due to the distinct probability that there was at least one decoy grave, and perhaps two. The English officials of the time would have been careful to see that the gravesite would not become a rallying-point for Irish nationalists. Our psychic respondents — who now numbered twenty-two — were describing three apparently different locations.

We decided to launch a psychic probe to find Emmet's **head**, since it was a matter of history that the head had been lost and the body buried headless. There would be no logical reason for a decoy head; confusion to our psychic respondents, therefore, would be minimal.

Armand again generously donated his time to this project. I provided him with a photo of Emmet's death mask, which was made before the head disappeared, and he chose June 23, 1982, as the most auspicious time (astrologically) to obtain valid information.

"Mercury's retrograding now," he explained, when asked on May 26 to participate in the probe. "When we're searching for something way back in the past, we'll have to do it when Mercury's going forward."

In the meantime, Armand meditated repeatedly on the photo of the death mask, and on June 23 we held the session.

"I definitely get this man being buried next to water, and a small stone bridge. There's no water now in the channel; it's dried up and the bottom is covered with small field stones. But the place is near water.

And the head is buried in a cemetery where the body's not too far from it, but it's in two different areas," Armand began. "Where the head is, it served as the floor of a building, a church or a religious chapel. I kept getting a lot of bodies, under the cement floor slabs. The building was connected to a house, I feel — a connecting vestibule, or whatever you call it.

"The head was placed in a catacomb-like. It was placed where there's nobility. In these catacombs... they buried the very noble or very elite.

"No matter how I tried to work on this, I kept getting that," said Armand, almost apologetically. "The head was placed where there was nobility buried. It could have been the mayor of the city or the 'princes' of the time, and there was also some very deep religious thing.

"And when you go there," he continued, "you will find an urn —. The head was placed in an urn. And it's in where there are persons of minor royalty buried. I see like it's closed up. It's been covered over, but I do get like it's still — somebody will remember it.

"There was a nobleman that really liked this man [Emmet], and he provided the burial for the head."

"Could you give me a name?" I asked.

"I keep getting like Herbert, or Herb, for a first name. And I keep getting an E-L, the last name. There's an H, and an E-L — Elshure, or Elsure, or Eliza, or — it's E-L-L-I-Z, something. It's not a ranking thing, but he had a title of some kind. They were close friends, and he provided the burial for this man. And they decided to part, you know, break his body up, separate the body, because I kept getting violence. They were afraid the body would be taken, or something.

"The urn," Armand continued, "I kept getting like there are lions' paws holding it up. It's round and it has a cap to it that's thick, and there's a lion's head, you know, like the lion's on its back and the mouth's open."

Armand sketched the "urn" he was perceiving as I asked what color it was.

"Well, it's awfully gray now and very dusty. It's like at one time they could have put flowers in it, and then they covered it. They put a cap on it. **His head is an urn** where the nobility are. I don't know if you can make sense of that or not."

"I'll certainly check it out," I promised.

And check it out we did. My daughter Allis Ann and I journeyed back to Dublin in mid-July, 1982. Among the thick files in my ever-present research bag were transcriptions of Armand's reading plus the transcripts of five triple-blind readings from psychic respondents of the Mobius Society.

The Mobius Society, a professional research group headquartered in Los Angeles, had become interested in the Emmet project in 1980. Its chairman of the board, Stephan A. Schwartz, recognized the search for Emmet's grave as a true, triple-blind situation — in other words, no one living on earth knew where the grave was located. It was the type of research where applied parapsychology could be best employed and the Mobius Group specializes in utilizing intuitively derived data in practical field research. Using blind protocol methodology, Mobius has been able to achieve substantial success, which has been reported in research papers at academic conferences and in numerous other literary sources.[22]

Mobius's contribution to this 1982 search for Emmet's head involved triple-blind perception by five of its talented psychics. The results had been fascinating — four of the five had circled, on an unidentified map, an area in and around Mt. Jerome Cemetery, south of the Dublin civic center, indicating that that area was related to the object of our search. They had chosen an area about one-third-mile square from a map depicting an area about sixty miles square. Correlation like this could not be ignored.

In addition, four had provided sketches of peculiar features associated with the location. Our team of six persons — Irish, English and American — searched the cemetery in question over a period of several days. All of the sketched features (some very unusual indeed — but that is a separate story) were found in the cemetery, centered in an area about two hundred feet square.

While following the features of a rough map which one of the Mobius respondents had sketched, I found, in the midst of the oldest part of the cemetery, a gray, dusty stone urn atop a grave. The urn was resting on lion's paws, and on each end was carved a magnificent lion's head, mouth open wide.

The urn was oblong rather than round, and the position of the paws and heads was different from those in Armand's sketch, but the coincidence could not be ignored. And the urn was situated on the site where one Mobius respondent had marked an "X," indicating where the object of our search would be found.

The urn showed definite signs of having been moved from an earlier site. Its stone top was tightly sealed. The area where it now rested was older than the cemetery itself; surrounding grave-stones carried dates twenty-five years older than the date when the graveyard was first established for public use.

The cemetery's head office — once the manor house of a rich gentleman — was about 200 feet away. Was this the location Armand had described — where an ancient graveyard and chapel had been connected in some manner to a large house of a nobleman?

The rich, influential Irishman, John Keogh, had sold this land, Mt. Jerome, shortly after 1830 to Dublin authorities in order that it might be used to provide a cemetery for Catholics. For centuries before 1830, the brutal penal laws imposed on Irish Catholics by their conquerors had forbidden formal burial to persons of that religious persuasion. Keogh himself was a Catholic, but rich, influential Catholics were a rare breed at that period in Irish history. Could he have secretly buried other Catholics on his own land before the Penal Laws were abolished?

Mt. Jerome, at that time, was surrounded by rushing rivers which flowed down each side of the low, rounded mount. This, too, fit in with Armand's reading. Lazy streams still flow there.

The authorities in the cemetery office could not explain why grave markers dated 1810 and 1811 were in the area near the urn. Neither could they explain why the grave onto which the lion-footed urn had evidently been moved long ago was that of a daughter of an Anglican minister. Although the cemetery is now nondenominational, in 1837 (the date of the grave in question), the cemetery was for Catholic burials only.

Since the urn clearly was not a sarcophagus and did not contain a recorded internment, I asked permission to open it. I was advised to contact the descendants, if any, of the family involved or, that failing, to seek permission from appropriate legal authorities.

At the present writing, permission will be granted to open the urn, but a set of conditions must be fulfilled before this is done. Eventually the urn will be opened in full view of Irish authorities. Armand and other psychics who have given readings on pictures of the gray stone urn predict that, within it, lies evidence of the location of Emmet's lost head and the location where persons unknown laid his headless body to rest.

CHAPTER NINE

"Developing Detective/Psychic Teams"

Throughout this book we have purposely kept the text in free-flowing narrative, to better illustrate the weird and spontaneous interplay in detective/psychic teamwork. For this final chapter, however, we will attempt to structure and caption our suggestions as to how police and psychics can work effectively together. Armand's own terminology and easy style, however, are also preserved here, and Dr. Louise Ludwig's wise words will be liberally interspersed.

Interaction between professional clairvoyants and those policemen who have already worked successfully together will probably differ, in varying degree, from those teams who are new at the experience, but hopefully the suggestions will benefit both groups. The chapter is particularly directed toward those who have never tried the procedure but are curious to find out how the process will work for them. It is also directed toward policemen and psychics who have been unsuccessful in the past, and who were discouraged by failure to discover how the process is best approached.

Like any scientific methodology, detective/psychic teamwork needs structuring and protocol to be most efficient. Such protocol has not yet been systematically determined. That is for the future. There are five clear statements we can make, however, which will enable interested persons to discover how such teams work best, and five specific techniques the participants can employ in order to learn and pursue these endeavors. The statements, and their explanations, are as follows:

I. THE DETECTIVE IS A PSYCHIC.

The first step in successful detective/psychic teamwork is the recognition by all parties that many detectives themselves are psychic to a degree, even though they may have no conscious awareness of the fact. Both Armand Marcotte and Dr. Ludwig emphasize this point.

"Basically, they do it subconsciously," explains Armand. "Detectives have inquisitive minds, and anyone with an inquisitive mind has some psychic ability. Anyone who can think for themselves, without misleading themselves, is psychic, for it means their subconscious mind is feeding information to their conscious mind.

"The police solve many cases, using their own curiosity, intelligence, "hunches," and by painstaking work. But in some cases the subconscious stops feeding information to the detectives' conscious minds, because they are not trained to receive beyond a certain stage.

"When they draw a blank wall, they should seek a psychic who understands the mechanics of psychic perception and therefore can help explore it further."

Dr. Ludwig, in turn, states, "No one has ever trained police officers **themselves** to use their psychic ability. Repair of this omission would perfect the most efficient use of psychic information, inasmuch as the officers know police procedures and requirements and would be readily accessible to and under the direct control of the police department."

In this way, the two main drawbacks to successful psychic detecting could be immediately remedied. Dr. Ludwig's seminars for law enforcement personnel are a step in that direction, but much work remains to be done in the future.

II. THE NEED FOR CONFIDENTIALITY IS ALL-IMPORTANT.

Throughout the preceding chapters the need for confidentiality has been stressed. We have used only sample cases where Armand's involvement has received publicity in the press and where he, himself, remained anonymous. The detectives involved in these cases were also quoted in the articles concerning their use of the psychic input.

Louise Ludwig explained why the need for confidentiality is so crucial. "For example," she states, "you're working on a case. The police don't have suspects, and you come up with a new line of investigation for them.

"In the meantime, the psychic may talk to the newspapers — which has happened. The detective's case is then disrupted by this information being made public, and the new suspect reads about **himself**. 'The police are looking for a person of such-and-such description, of this occupation, last seen at such-and-such a place,' and the suspect thinks, 'Oh, is that right? I guess I'll go to New Jersey!'

"When the Hillside Strangler case was going on in Los Angeles," she continues, "a particular psychic called up the LAPD office out at the west end, talked to the desk sergeant for about five minutes about the case — in other words, engaged **him** in conversation. **He** didn't want to talk. The next day she gave an interview to the papers saying she'd been consulted by the LAPD. When this sort of situation occurs, the police feel, rightfully, that they have been **used**. They are justified in getting angry.

"Then there's the legal point of view, where a psychic may compromise a case with the courts," explains Dr. Ludwig. "Any advance publicity about a case that could in any way sway a juror's mind is something the police want to avoid. And there's also the question of 'admissible evidence.' "

As was explained in Chapter Four, psychics rarely come up with information that is admissible in court; they usually only supply new leads, or advise the investigating officers to go back and recheck some aspect they've forgotten or dropped as inconsequential.

When the detective **does** use psychic input and comes up with verifiable information against a particular suspect, that **is** admissible in court. The psychic **impressions** were not.

The problem here is how to establish legally that the officer had "probable cause" to retrace his steps and verify the information. Most times, if the court knows the lead first came from a psychic, the evidence will be ruled against even though it was verified later. This is the second reason why the use of psychics must be kept confidential.

"Information that psychics give usually will not meet the requirements of 'probable cause,' " states Louise Ludwig. "But take the case, for example, where a psychic brought out information about a safe-deposit box where incriminating evidence would be found against a suspect. This would be directly involved in 'probable cause,' for the police, in asking permission for a search warrant to open that box, would have to reveal that only the psychic initially knew of the existence of the safe-deposit box. There are only rare instances where a judge would rule psychic information 'probable cause.' "

Gradually, however, as in the Southgate, California case discussed briefly in Chapter Four, courts are beginning to accept action by police under the legal definition of "probable cause," even though the information was first obtained through psychic channels.[23]

Because of these two sound reasons for confidentiality, the detectives involved in the four sample cases could not be interviewed for this book. Gradually, however, the use of psychics in police work will become more established and methodical, and the situation will change to suit the needs of the community.

III. THE PSYCHIC PROCESS IS BEST DONE WITH PERSONS NOT EMOTIONALLY INVOLVED IN THE CRIME.

Relatives and friends of murdered and missing persons emit excessive emotion which clouds a psychic's perceptual channels. For this reason, both Armand and Dr. Ludwig prefer to work directly with detectives, rather than through the families of the victims.

"If you're working on a police case that is very gruesome, you can't be afraid to bring out the details. If a relative were present, you'd hesitate, and this would affect the free flow of information. But the detective would already know at least some of the details, and, anyway, he's trained to be objective. Therefore, a psychic, working like this, can just tell it like it was," states Armand, who has had several involvements in this type of problem.

"If your vision indicates that the victim had a problem, whether it was a dual personality or a sexual perversion or whatever, you should stress that and stick to it. Relatives, if present, would often not be able to accept the answers you give them, and would feed false information back to you. It wouldn't be their fault and wouldn't be a deliberate dishonesty, but it still clouds the psychic vision. That's why you should be with a person who **knows** the victim in the sense that he is involved directly in the investigation, but who has no emotional involvement or hangups over the walk of life that person was in at the time of death."

The psychic, too, must be nonemotionally involved in the crime. As Armand states, they have to understand their **own** emotions and in particular must understand that they are not doing this type of work for any benefit to themselves. They are working for the benefit of others.

"They must always keep an open mind," advised Armand, "because anytime they close their minds to anything that might come to them, it will only close off their own enlightenment. A psychic's personal emotions shouldn't enter into it at all. He should be objective, for this aids the relaxation process. Both individuals should go into it with an open mind, and the research should be done afterwards, by the detective, to prove out any of the messages that come through."

In regard to personal emotions of psychics, Dr. Ludwig's proposed training sessions (see below) would also instruct psychics how to curb the tendency toward vanity. As a group, Dr. Ludwig states, sensitives (psychics) tend to be somewhat insecure and typically compensate for this with vanity and envy of other sensitives.

Dr. Ludwig also prefers not to work with relatives. "It's more objective; that can be our biggest reason. Because it's really very difficult for everybody — the victims and all. When PsiCom first began working on police cases, about February 1978, we involved relatives in the process, but we've changed that now."

In contrast to Armand, PsiCom prefers to work with an officer who is **not** connected with the investigation of that particular crime.

"We'd rather have police departments send us an officer who doesn't know anything about the case. Theoretically, that way we won't be reading his mind and telling him back what he already knows" explains Louise.

"But the fact that we might be reading the mind of the officer in charge, even if he's five hundred miles away, adds a lot of complications in trying to sort out what is accurate and what **might** be accurate. In my opinion, the only way you can ever know what is accurate is after you've checked it out in reality and found it to be true."

IV. HONEST INTERCHANGE IS NECESSARY BETWEEN MEMBERS OF DETECTIVE/PSYCHIC TEAMS.

Honest exchange of information between detectives and psychics brings about the most valid results. Conversely, deliberate deception on the part of the detective can mar psychic vision, just as impure motives on the part of the sensitives can interfere with the crime-solving process.

"If detectives, for any reason, mislead a psychic and give him or her false information, they bring impurity to the psychic vision," explains Armand. "And with impurity come dark or evil forces, which misguide the psychic. Psychics must always be of a pure mind. They have to be honest, just like the detective must be. They have to want to do this work for the good of society, and not for building up their own reputations or any other impure motive.

"Whenever a policeman (or **any** individual) misleads a psychic, that person always gets a bad reading. If you have a doubting Thomas, for instance, you're going to be led astray.

"The detective can be skeptical, but it has to be an honest skepticism. As a rule, when a detective comes to me, he **wants** to believe, at least partially — otherwise, they wouldn't be there.

"Sometimes the misleading information can be entirely innocent. This is what happened with Detective Costas on the Casaneda case. I told him, 'You interviewed a man,' and I gave him the name. 'He's the murderer but you let him go.'

"Detective Costas kept saying, 'I didn't interview this man', and I said, 'You go back and check your records.' And he did, and found he **had** interviewed him, and that I was right. It was just like when he thought the male victim's eyes were brown. I told him they were hazel, and he checked that out, too, with the coroner's report. [See Chapter Two]

"Now that was an honest mistake on the detective's part, so it didn't clog my vision. But a mistake made purposely will definitely allow the dark forces to come in."

By "dark forces" Armand means two different things. One is the evil that is contrary to good. "You see, there's good and evil in all of us," he states. "When one person is trying to deceive the other, the evil brings evil, just like good brings good."

On the rare occasions when he has met deliberate deception, Armand finds out **after the reading** that this has occurred. He perceives deception during the reading, but if the person involved keeps assuring him that the false information is true, his confidence in his own perception slips, and he is likely to give false information in return.

"You **know** it — you **feel** it. You know there's something wrong, but you can't put your finger on it. Finally, even though you **feel** it's wrong, you say to yourself, 'well, he knows what he's talking about. He's the detective, and he's doing the investigation.' "

Occasionally, however, the evil forces which enter in when the psychic is fed false information are more than "created" evil or evil in general, as opposed to good. Sometimes the evil is in the form of dark intelligences — spirits akin to what some Western religions call demons. Armand advises all psychics to protect themselves by calling upon the Supreme Good (God), so these evil intelligences cannot influence them in any way. On occasion, dark spiritual forces like these can enter the body of the psychic and cause dual personalities or other types of emotional damage.

Armand allows spirits of the victims of crime to enter his body only partially in order to make limited use of his vocal cords, for example, but only after he protects himself spiritually. He cautions psychics who are in the learning process not to fool around with mediumship (communication with spirits in either full or partial trance) without the guidance of highly evolved, wise teachers. Simple remote viewing is best for the beginner and the untrained psychic. (See under Techniques in this chapter.)

V. THE MOON HAS A ROLE IN CRIME AND CRIME-SOLVING.

It is an established fact that the moon somehow affects the crime rate. Scientific studies done on this intriguing situation indicate that the number of violent crimes, such as murders, rapes, and other types of severe assaults rise sharply at the time of a full moon. The reason for this has not been scientifically established.[24]

"When it's a full moon," Armand says, "it brings about all the emotions of people to their fullest. And if those emotions are evil, then the result is destructive; if they're constructive emotions, the result is very constructive.

"You see, the full moon fulfills a promise. It will fulfill whatever was meant to fulfilled. It can also influence psychic readings on crime, because the psychic is more sensitive at the time of a full moon. And, for instance, if the crime was committed during a full moon, like Raymond's murder was [Chapter Seven], if you can get a reading at the full moon, you can recapture it more accurately and in much more detail than if you give it when the moon is decreasing. That's because you get all the emotions involved. If you give the reading at any other time of the month, you don't seem to get so much out of it."

Armand also suggests that new projects should be started, and finished, according to the phases of the moon. This could, logically, apply also to various phases of psychic detecting, whenever possible.

"I do better when the moon is heavy [full], but if I begin a new project on a new moon, it makes an auspicious beginning. And then, as the moon gets full, you fulfill your vision. On a new moon, you start, and then at the full moon you visualize your finished product.

"For example, if you wanted to advertise for household help, you advertise when it's a new moon — then by the full moon you have the right person."

Similarly, this book was started (first planned) on the date of a new moon, although at the time this writer (Druffel) did not realize it. Armand had planned it that way. It was finished in the last days of January, 1983 when the winter moon hung heavy in the sky. By that time I had learned to listen to Armand's advice!

As stated above, we offer five specific techniques the participants in detective/psychic teamwork might gainfully employ. Those techniques are as follows:

I. ADVANTAGEOUS TIMES FOR USE OF THE PSYCHIC METHODOLOGY.

Psychic detecting, in the past, has been mostly a hit-or-miss process, with detectives contacting psychics sometimes years after the clues and leads had run out or in cases, as Dr. Ludwig describes, of "desperation."

Armand advises police to contact their psychics within two weeks of the crime, rather than waiting two or three years, as they often do when bringing cases to him.

"If they come up against a block, they should come within two weeks," he states. "If they're on the track of solving the crime themselves, they don't need us. But on the unresolved crimes, if they draw a blank and need added clues, leads or other input, then they should come to us."

He specifies two weeks because that gives the detective time to gather enough information so that the crime scene has been fully scoured and all material and verbal evidence elicited from witnesses, possible suspects and other interested persons. If the case is **too** fresh, the police might not have enough verified information to bear out what the psychic might perceive about the crime and might tend to disregard something he or she says that could actually hold the key to solving the crime.

"There's really no set time when the police should come to us," Armand summarizes. "Because most of the time they already know who did it — they just have to prove it. But in cases where they're baffled — they've done all this research, and there's nowhere to go — they should seek out a psychic who can help open up new doors and new avenues of investigation."

II. PROPER RESPONSES TO PSYCHIC READINGS.

Both Armand Marcotte and Dr. Ludwig stress the necessity of

established protocol or rules of procedure in detective/psychic team-work. Armand's main rule is that a psychometric object must be brought. With the help of training courses such as those offered by PsiCom, additional rules for both psychics and police will eventually be established.

"The psychics themselves, ideally, could be trained to report information in ways most useful for police work and in the use of standardized nomenclature by which to give precise, detailed physical descriptions," states Dr. Ludwig. However, this lies in the future, when such use of psychics will be openly accepted by police, courts and public alike.

In the meantime, general rules of thumb are emerging:

(1) That only detectives willing to believe, at least partially, in the psychic method be employed in such teams, for the reasons put forth in State-ment IV, above, "HONEST INTERCHANGE OF INFORMATION..."

(2) That the psychic be permitted to lay his own ground rules governing verbal response during his reading. For example, Armand prefers silence during his meditation and initial work with the psychometric object. Silence aids his relaxation. Unexpected movements or noises, such as the scraping of chair legs across the floor, also upset his concentration.

(3) That the number of police representatives present at a reading be in accord with the psychic's wishes. For example, Armand prefers that a detective who has been directly involved with the crime since the beginning come alone for the session. He feels that the spirit of the murder victim is aware that this detective is most anxious to solve the crime. Even the detective's partner is asked to wait out-side during the reading, for, as Armand explains, the presence of an added person's vibrations clouds his perceptions of the matter at hand.

(4) When the perceptions about the crime start flowing freely, Armand begins to describe what he sees or hears happening on the crime scene. A tape recorder should be used at this point, for Armand, at this stage, is not always wholly aware of what is happening and often cannot recall parts of what he has said.

Since much perceptual material is symbolic or clothed in raw data form (geometric shapes, etc.), some of what he says cannot be interpreted immediately. In this event, it is wise for the detective to remain silent or to accept the status quo, whether or not he accepts the statements as valid. A good example of this was in the Casaneda case, where Armand perceived the crime location as a "hotel" and the passage leading to the rooms as a "hallway without lights." Detective Costas, in this instance, had the intuitional knowledge to recognize that Armand was seeing the building in raw data form, that is, it was in reality a motel whose passage between the rooms consisted of an open-air walk beneath a darkened sky. If Costas had said, "That's wrong" when Armand spoke of the hotel with unlighted halls, the psychic's further perceptions might have been tinged with doubt or blanked out entirely, due to a misleading statement by the detective.

(5) Armand requests the detectives who use his services to indicate by short, positive phrases when the material he is describing is accurate, according to their knowledge of the cases. He prefers phrases like, "That's right", or "Go on." These encourage him to know he's on the right track, and the confidence aids further perceptions to flow.

When he reaches a flow of information relating to events the detective does **not** know and which are linked to possible solutions of the crime, Armand prefers them to say, "More detail, please" or something akin to that. This gives him the assurance that the information he is relaying seems linked to the crime and might provide clues or leads which will aid the detective in his investigation.

(6) In general, during the reading the psychic should be given free rein to talk, write or sketch, rather than impart his perceptions in a conversation-like dialogue. Any questions or comments made to a psychic during a session should be free of any need for logic or intellectualizing. The right-brain hemisphere from which psychic data flows resists attempts at analysis. Its data is essentially unfiltered and is best unhampered by language logic, mathematics or other formal intellectualization.[25] Of course, the psychics must use language in describing what they envision, but they must be free to choose the terminology in which they describe their perceptions. Some of the data is very hard to describe — it is more in the area of feelings. When this happens, the psychic must not feel forced to verbalize it precisely if unable to do so. In regard to this, detectives may be surprised how much of the tape-recorded information makes sense **after** the session, when the tapes are transcribed and reviewed. As an example, this writer (Druffel) did not fully understand all the implications of Armand's reading on the skeleton in the basement (Chapter Eight) until days later. A subconscious process may be at work here on the part of the recipient of the information (the detective) — a process little understood, but

nevertheless valuable.

(7) Above all, states Armand, "If a detective comes with a case and he's open to the psychic method, then it can be solved. But if he comes with a lot of negative thinking, then it can't.

"I'd rather have one that says, 'Look, I don't believe in anything like this, but I'll **help** you, and **mean** it. Then I **know** it will work."

III. TRAINING IN PSYCHIC METHODS.

Dr. Ludwig has proposed the idea of instituting training sessions — participants to be composed of police officers who wish to develop their own psychic abilities and/or those who wish to learn how to work effectively with psychics.[26]

These sessions would teach the officers to separate rational thinking from psychic impressions (left-right brain hemisphere perception, see Chapter Five) and to learn correct focusing, that is, how to eliminate contaminating psychic impressions from unrelated persons and events from psychic information about suspects and victims.

For these training sessions, Dr. Ludwig would organize and supervise all instruction and would request police assistance in:

(1) recruitment of officer-sensitives;
(2) feedback on participants' performances;
(3) psychometric objects — some related to actual crimes and some not related — for training and practice.

Dr. Ludwig invites police officers to inquire, if interested, by writing to PsiCom, P.O. Box 75583, Los Angeles, CA 90075.

"The police can also learn to distinguish between those psychics who have something to offer and those who are charlatans" she states. "They can begin to start searching for somebody they can **really** trust, who will maintain professional confidentiality. They can begin trying them out, giving them a trial run to see if they really keep their mouths shut or if 'they're just another crazy.' Officers have legitimate doubts about psychics. I don't blame them; I can understand.

"Psychics and police officers, at this time, do not understand how the other one works. The police have been burned by unscrupulous psychics, out after money or publicity. A professional approach is what is needed."

Until this professional approach is generally accepted, however, the following specific psychic techniques can be learned and employed by beginners or psychics who already have recognized their talents but have not yet disciplined them to the point of reliability.

They can also be used by **anyone** who is curious to know whether or not they have trainable ability. It is very possible that some degree of psychic ability is universal. The specific techniques, each of which will be discussed in turn, are:

(1) Relaxation;
(2) Remote-viewing;
(3) Psychometry;
(4) Dream analysis;
(5) Back-up metaphysical studies.

1. Relaxation

Whether the training is done individually or in groups, the ability to relax body and mind is the first step to psychic perceptions. Almost without exception, spontaneous psychic incidents occur when the unwary percipient is in a relaxed state. The relaxation can range from full sleep, to the twilight zone between sleep and awakening, to daydreaming, to times when the percipient was engaged in humdrum tasks or quiet hobbies.

Why a relaxed state seems necessary to psychic perception is not scientifically understood, but it is assumed that the information in the subconscious mind (or reaching the subconscious mind from an outside source) can penetrate into the conscious mind more easily if the conscious part of the mind is at rest.

Armand advises his students to purposely shut off everyday problems or any thought concerned with everyday living. A comfortable position is essential, and the body must not be aware of cold or excessive heat, or urgent physical demands such as hunger, thirst, persistent coughs, tight clothing, etc.

Sounds from the environment should be minimized. This is one of the main reasons why groups should meet weekly at the same place at the same time. Groups should choose an environs free of demands from family, pets, neighbors, etc. Muffle the phone. In other words, the surroundings should be as peaceful and tranquil as possible. Any sounds which cannot be silenced, such as barking dogs, should be familiar to the members of the group or individual;

any necessary noise should not require attention by members of the group.

Different individuals have different means of relaxing. For some, a warm cup of coffee quiets the mind, but for others it wires the body to a disquiet pitch. For some, a cigarette aids relaxation; for others, cigarette smoke produces allergies and other physical distress. Differing preliminary relaxation methods must be compatible within the group.

Autohypnosis is a convenient and simple way to bring about the state of relaxation necessary for psychic perception, but it is not necessary. There are many scientifically written books on this technique.

Some persons with strong psychic powers are able to slip into a state akin to (but not necessarily identical with) what Armand describes as the "grayed twilight zone" which begins his readings. (See Chapter Five) This, however, is not necessary for successful psychic perception; the relaxation state is as individual as the human beings themselves.

2. Remote-viewing

The term "remote-viewing" or "remote-sensing" came into scientific favor with the work done by Dr. Russell Targ and Dr. Harold Puthoff of the SRI, International in Menlo Park, California. Their work is historically and scientifically intriguing, for it first demonstrated, in experiments convincing to many scientists, the ability of the ordinary person to perceive psychically.

Targ and Puthoff's book, *Mind Reach*, published in 1977, gives explicit instructions which enable almost anyone to duplicate their success.[27]

To reduce "remote-viewing" to simple components, the percipient (one who was to receive psychic impressions of a so-called "target" area) had no knowledge of what the targets were to be. Neither did the lab assistant who remained with the percipient record the results. The targets were chosen at random by another team, who proceeded to the target areas. At a predetermined time, the percipient was instructed to "relax" and let information come into his mind about the area where the other team was. The percipient sketched various details (geometric shapes and other unfiltered data) without trying to intellectualize about their meaning. If information about a specific building or area — or perhaps a name — came spontaneously, through inner sight, hearing, feeling or other sense modalities, this was to be recorded, but logic and guessing were to play no part. Later, the percipient's sketch was compared to the features at the target area by independent judges, who determined the degree of correlation.

The results of remote-viewing, whether in laboratory experiments or in private sessions, will demonstrate to any open-minded person that a part of the human mind is capable of perceiving information without the use of the five physical senses. It is basically this technique — whether called remote-viewing or any other name — which can be learned by those interested in psychic detecting.

Groups might first experiment with names of people or locations in a sealed envelope, where only one member of the group knows the answer, such as described in Chapter Four. Or a person not associated with the group can make up envelopes with names of well-known persons or places, and these sealed envelopes can be used at the group sessions. Names and locations containing high emotional content seem to work best in this type experiment.

Another experiment used by Armand in his teaching sessions is to have each member "forecast" what will happen within the next week, month, etc., to other members of the group. As in all group experiments, records should be carefully kept, and as to the events "forecast" occur, they should be noted.

Objects, of high emotional content if possible, can also be brought to the session in sealed boxes, and remote-viewing processes used to perceive impressions as to the object inside.

3. Psychometry

Learning the technique of psychometry is probably vital to developing psychic talent for police work. It is the technique favored by both Armand and PsiCom. Most psychic sessions with detectives involve the psychometrizing of an object intimately connected with the victim. The closer the association the object has to victim and crime, the more successful these sessions are. Virtually every successful clairvoyant who has assisted police in crime solving has been aided by the use of psychometric objects.

The term psychometry usually means physical handling of the object by the percipients. Some psychics merely touch or hold the object lightly; others stroke or rub portions of it; some "wring" the object (if it is pliable) as if squeezing information from it. The most important thing to remember about learning the technique is that the handling is done while in the relaxed state and while "remotely-viewing" or otherwise perceiving impressions about the object and the person to whom it belonged

The objects used in practice sessions may range from photographs to samples of handwriting to pieces of clothing and jewelry. Objects with great emotional content are best. If possible, use photos, handwriting and clothing/jewelry from the same individual in learning sessions. The more psychometric objects that refer back to the source that is being perceived, the better the impressions will flow. Armand asks detectives to bring him a number of objects from the crime scene or from the murder victim — the more the better.

Professional psychics who work with police differ widely in the types of psychometric objects used or preferred. For some, a simple snapshot of the crime scene may trigger valid perceptions, whereby another does best by handling the weapon with which the murder was committed. If photos are used, original or negatives are best, as they are "closer" to the actual crime that a print made from a copy negative, for example. Some psychics hold the photos and draw impressions without looking at them; others work best by gazing at the photos and letting peripheral images flow in.

We reiterate Armand's philosophy about psychometric objects here. "It's like a good surgeon or any other good tradesman," he explains. "He needs **material** to work with. A good psychic cannot just draw things from the air. He needs an object to work with that is of concern to the detective. The object helps bring on the trance state I work in, because it's a link to the victim's time track. Once that is established, I can go on and explore from there."

Dr. Ludwig states that she does not know how the psychic data is derived from psychometric objects. "Actually, there are hypotheses about this. I don't know whether the object simply forms a 'bridge' to that person, or if something of that person is actually attached to the object, or if it's some other way altogether. Whatever it is, I **do** know it seems to me that we work better with an object than if we're just **told** about a person, like, 'Will you please tell us about Joe Smith, who used to live in Kalamazoo.' We're more accurate when we have an object. Whether that object simply gives us confidence of the fact that we are in connection with that person in some way — that may be all that it's doing."

If the psychometric experimentation is part of official police-training sessions, actual objects from crime scenes may be made available. These, of course, will have full emotional content and probably give more and truer impressions, even to a beginner.

The general information sought from a psychometric object involves the gender, age and physical description of the person to whom it is associated. Other information would be occupation, physical description, location of home, state of health, family makeup, physical or psychological idiosyncrasies, ad infinitum. Whatever impressions come should be recorded, no matter if they seem strange, gruesome or otherwise unpalatable. The psychics should remain open to all impressions which may flow spontaneously from the object into their minds.

In psychometry training sessions, as in all other phases of detective/psychic teamwork, every percipient should make every effort to avoid negative emotions, such as jealousy or envy of other members who may seem to be more talented, and conversely, avoidance of vanity and discrimination toward those who seem to be less talented. In Armand's philosophy, it is wise to feel that we are put on this earth to help each other willingly and that each person has a rightful place in the Universe.

Dedication, patience and time are the watchwords to a successful training period. Professional psychics — even those whose talents were apparent from childhood, as were Armand's — devote years to study, experiments and practice. If studying in a group, each member should reserve that particular time weekly and let nothing interfere with it. Progress will be painfully slow at times — positive thinking should be employed always.

Armand feels that the members, either privately or in concert, should begin and end each session with a meditation directed toward the Supreme Good (God). Protection from evil influences should also be requested. This is especially important when handling objects associated with actual crimes, as such objects apparently hold and bring forth impressions of the evil inherent in the crime. The PsiCom group however does not use meditative techniques.

4. Dream Analysis

Dreams are symbolized information from the subconscious areas of the human mind. They can be considered a potential reservoir of knowledge about things we cannot know through ordinary means.

One of PsiCom's members, (see Chapter Four), following detective/psychic sessions, often dreams information relating to those particular crimes which were discussed.

Dreams can be analyzed by anyone who takes the time, patience, and energy to do so. There are many scientific books written on the subject. One of the best written for the layman is *Working With Dreams*, by Montague Ullmann, M.D., and Nan Zimmerman.[28]

We will not go into this subject here, other than to point out that dream analysis can be a valuable technique in this field.

5. Backup Metaphysical Studies

The lay person is not restricted to "scientific methods," such as remote-viewing, psychometry and dream analysis in developing psychic skills. Perhaps professional policemen would prefer to restrict their studies to those which are being discussed in academic journals, as the members of PsiCom do, but others interested in developing psychic talents for police teamwork need not necessarily do this. They are free to explore the skills of palmistry, astrology, numerology and other so-called "occult" studies. As was discussed in Chapter Five, Armand uses astrological information as a "backup" to his psychical perceptions and he encourages his students to study any branch of metaphysics in which they have particular interest. Whether or not the skill is used as a separate backup method or simply as a "link" in remote-and-psychometric perception depends entirely on the individual.

The important point to stress here is that the use of backup skills, even though not convincing to scientific types and professional police, does not take away from the reliability of information from a truly talented psychic. These "occult" skills are not in any way connected to the called "black arts." What is being sought is verifiable information; how it is derived is beside the question.

IV. MEDITATION AND DIET.

The role of diet in psychic ability has been fairly well established. Here the adage "a sound mind in a sound body" can include "a sound ability to perceive psychically.' Armand's diet has already been discussed in Chapter Five.

It is a striking fact that the majority of good psychics **do** recognize that their food intake affects their abilities — the general attitude is that light foods help raise the vibratory rate of the body, making it, supposedly, closer to the vibrations of the dimension from which psychic impressions flow. In general (though there are exceptions), the more professional and reliable a clairvoyant is, the more the tendency to diet and fast according to self-prescribed rules. It is assumed that each psychic will establish his or her own rules of diet, intake of alcohol, smoking, etc., and do what seems to work best for him or her.

Meditation and psychic faculties have, likewise, been inextricably linked throughout the recorded history of humankind. Each psychic must choose their own meditative technique, as well as their own definition. "Meditation," to some persons means silent prayer; to others it means contemplation of the inner self; to others, it is immersion in the immensity of the Universe.

Armand's meditative technique involves quiet, peace and tranquillity, found within the confines of his own home and office surroundings. His meditations, however, include prayer to Almighty God for protection as well as help and guidance.

V. AVOIDING PITFALLS AND REAPING REWARDS OF DETECTIVE/PSYCHIC TEAMWORK.

Finally, we must speak of the pitfalls which await the unwary entrants into this type of work, and then finish on an optimistic note, discussing the rewards (nonfinancial!) which can come to those who enter this field.

The main pitfall to a psychic is being misled by a person who comes ostensibly seeking help in crime-solving. On rare occasions, a skeptical or antagonistic detective will try to mislead for the purpose of "proving" the psychic method does not work. As Armand makes clear in Chapter Five, this type of deception is not always perceived clearly by the psychic, but the result is almost invariably an unfruitful session.

There is also the danger, as Armand describes, of a psychic

"becoming too cocky" if his reliability is such that detectives start seeking his services. An attitude of true humility is always best — a recognition that the psychic talents come from our Creator, and not from ourselves. They should, he feels, be used to serve others, not the psychics themselves. A staunch decision not to profit financially from such work will aid the common good, and help prevent any tendency to vanity.

Another pitfall, according to Armand's experience, is entering into a session without being at perfect peace or ease. "Never start, and then have to leave to go here or there," he advises. "Too many things coming in on us from the outside, the live-in-world material — that's a major stumbling block. A phone rings, you have to go someplace — and you lose the contact then. **You can never regain that original contact.**

"If you are interrupted, or the detective doesn't tape it or otherwise doesn't get out of it everything he needs, you can't recapture it. The next readings are always something else. Your first impression is always your best one, and you can't recapture it. You can only add to it.

"I think it's because in a certain time you are **meant** to recapture it. And other times you're not. It's just like a writer writes something today, and a week later he goes back to it. You can't write it identically, unless you read it back. There's no way you could do that."

What Armand says about the similarity of writing and psychic impressions is very true. Many writers get their best ideas, paragraphs, dialogue, etc., when their subconscious is most active, oftentimes waking up in the middle of the night with material for pages of manuscript literally flowing into their minds. These writers have learned to get up immediately and write the words as they come — for if they wait until the next morning, marvelous ideas have been forgotten and cannot be recaptured.

"The same thing happens sometimes after a detective has left — I get added information," explains Armand. "For example, in the Casaneda case, after the policeman left, the man's spirit started blasting away. He wouldn't give information while the detective was there, because he still hated the law, but he came through when I was alone. I didn't have a tape recorder and so I wrote down everything I got from him immediately, because I **knew** I couldn't retain it. Then I called the detective and told him. It's the same way with almost any reading. There are very few where I retain the details of what I've gotten."

Armand feels the spiritual reward for those psychics who enter this field involves a feeling of being closer to God. It is connected with the idea that the psychic and the detective help the victims find peace.

"In this work, I help a spirit reach a plateau where he receives the justice he is seeking. When the spirit of a crime victim has made the facts of the crime public, and the criminal is caught, then that soul can rest in peace. It's like a release from bondage.

"The person often has to prove that **he or she** didn't bring about the crime, but that it was brought on through a past incarnation and concerned a *karmic* debt that had to be paid. The psychics bring this reward of peace to the victim's soul, and **their** reward is the service of the common good."

Armand does not feel all murdered persons whose crimes haven't been solved are still hovering around in the earth plane. Many times the crime, and *karmic* debt, are resolved by the criminal himself dying.

To use an ancient example, the spirit of the man whose skeleton was found in St. Catherine's basement (see Chapter Eight), in Armand's opinion, probably found peace when the older man who killed him met his own death later on. At that point, the psychic states, justice came and both were released, to be returned to other life cycles to sort out their differences.

"You're allowed a certain time on earth," he reiterates, "and in that time, if you cause yourself to be killed, then you're earthbound until that time is over with, or until the person is caught or confesses to it — accepts the guilt. That releases the soul to higher incarnation. But until that person admits to the guilt, the judgment hasn't come for both of them."

Armand makes clear that he is speaking from his own philosophical understanding. He does not pretend that his thinking is the only theological interpretation or the last word.

In summary, therefore, as crime statistics mushroom to unprecedented heights, the scientific methods employed by law enforcement officials have become more and more ingenious. Yet the criminals seem to be winning the battle.

Peace officers, however, can use the psychic method to ferret out perpetrators of violent crimes. This method is still on the fringes of science, but as its protocol and scientific methodology become established and widely used, it can turn out to be an effective deterrent to crime. Criminals will think twice before committing violent acts, for they will be up against most unusual adversaries — detective/psychic teams who have the ability to gain verifiable information through telepathic and other psychic processes. In other words, they will be able to pull out information from a Cosmic Mind.

REFERENCES AND NOTES

The references below are suggested as supplemental reading for those readers who wish to research further the various theories and hypotheses mentioned and noted by number in the text:

1. Puthoff, Harold and Russell Targ. "A Perceptual Channel for Information Transfer Over Kilometer Distances: Historical Perspective and Recent Research," *Proceedings of the IEEE*, Vol. 64, No. 3, March 1976: 329-356.
2. In Dr. Ludwig's experience, a good psychic on an average day may attain 25 to 30 percent accuracy. On a good day, he or she may approach 50 percent. The 80 to 85 percent figure, describing the accuracy of an exceptional psychic on an exceptional day, is generally recognized as a "working statistic" in the field of psychic research.
3 Hisey, Hehmann. *Keys to Inner Space*. New York: Avon Books, 1974. A comprehensive layman's book on occult studies.
4. Crookes, Sir William. *Researches in the Phenomena of Spiritualism*. London: Burns, 1874. One of the early objectively written books on the subject of mediumship. Also,

   Rogo, D. Scott. *Parapsychology: A Century of Progress*. New York: Taplinger Publishing Co., 1975.
5. Schwartz, Stephan A. *The Secret Vaults of Time*. New York: Grosset & Dunlap, 1978.
6. Crenshaw, James. "Court Admits Psychic Evidence," *Fate* Magazine, November 1979: 46-54.
7. Bucke, Richard Maurice. *Cosmic Consciousness*. New York: E. P. Dutton & Co., 1962.
8. Puthoff, Harold and Russell Targ. See Reference #1 above, esp. pages 349-350. Also,

   Mattack, Richard. "A Crude Model of the Mind-Matter Interaction Using Boha-Bub Hidden Variables," Physics Laboratory 1, H. C. Orsted Institute, University of Copenhagen, Copenhagen. An unpublished paper.
9. Muldoon, Sylvan and Hereward Carrington. *The Projection of the Astral Body*. New York: Samuel Weiser, 1970. A popular book on out-of-body experiences.
10. Krippner, Stanley, ed. *Extrasensory Perception*. New York: Plenum, 1978.
11. Tart, Charles, Harold Puthoff and Russell Targ. *Mind at Large*. New York: Praeger, 1979.
12. Moody, Raymond. *Life After Life*. Toronto, New York, London & Sydney: Bantam Books, 1975. Discussions of "life review" at death.

13. McBrien, Richard P. *Catholicism*. Minneapolis: Winston Press, 1980.
14. McBrien, Richard P. See Reference #13 above. Denies idea of reincarnation, but see:
    Stevenson, Ian. "Twenty Cases Suggestive of Reincarnation." New York: American Society for Psychic Research, 1966.
15. Puharich, Andrija. *Uri*. New York: Anchor Press, Doubleday and Company, Inc., 1974.
16. The near-death experience (NDE) is the subject of many cautious scientific inquiries at present, such as:
    Ring, Kenneth. *Life at Death: The Scientific Investigation of the Near-Death Experience*. New York: Coward, McCann and Goeghegan, 1980. Also,
    Sabom, Michael B. *Recollections of Death: A Medical Investigation*, New York, Harper and Row, 1981.
17. Hasted and Isaacs, eds. *Proceedings of the Parapsychology Association, 1982*. New Jersey: Scarecrow Press, 1983.
18. Fiore, Dr. Edith. *You Have Been Here Before*. New York: Coward, McCann & Geoghegan, Inc., 1978.
19. A branch of parapsychology studies the reception of paranormal voices via electronic communication devices, such as tape recorders, TV, telephones, intercom systems, radio, etc. The first paper-letter on tape-recorded voices was:
    Bayless, Raymond. "Correspondence" Section, *American Society for Psychic Research Journal*, January 1959, Vol. LIII, No. 1: 35-38. Also,
    Welch, William A. *Talks with the Dead*. New York: Pinnacle Books, Inc., 1975. Also,
    Roudive, Konstantin. *Breakthrough*. New York: Taplinger Publishing Co., 1971.
20. Landreth, Helen. *Pursuit of Robert Emmet*. New York-London: Whittlesey House, McGraw-Hill Book Company, Inc., 1948.
21. Druffel, Ann. "The Search for an Irish Martyr," Parts I and II, *Fate* Magazine, November and December 1979: 58-64, 82-88.
22. Schwartz, Stephan A. "A Prototype Applied Parapsychological Methodology for Utilization in Archeology," *Proceedings of the Parapsychological Association*. New Jersey: Scarecrow Press, 1982.
23. Crenshaw, James. See Reference #6.
24. "Moon Madness No Myth," in Mind-Body Section, *Science Digest*, Vol. 89, No. 2, March 1981: 106.
25. Krippner, Stanley. See Reference #10 above.

26. Reiser, M. and L. Ludwig, et al. "An Evaluation of the Use of Psychics in the Investigation of Major Crimes," *Journal of Police Science and Administration*, March 1979. A landmark paper in the field of detective/psychic work.
27. Targ, Russell and Harold Puthoff. *Mind-Reach*. New York: Delacorte Press/Eleanor Friede, 1977.
28. Ullman, Montague, M.D., and Nan Zimmerman. *Working with Dreams*. New York: Dell/Eleanor Friede, 1979.

INDEX

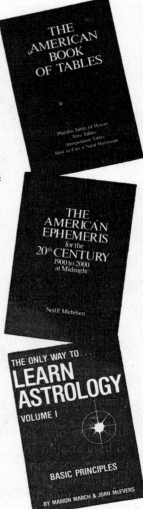

We calculate. . . You delineate!

CHART CALCULATIONS

Natal Chart wheel with planet/sign glyphs. Choice of house system: Placidus (standard), Equal, Koch, Campanus, Meridian, Porphyry, Regiomontanus, Topocentric, or Alcabitius. Choice of tropical (standard) or sidereal zodiac. Aspects, elements, planetary nodes, declinations, midpoints, etc. . 2.00

Arabic Parts All traditional parts and more 1.00

Asteroids ⚳ ⚴ ⚵ ⚶ in wheel + aspects/midpoints .50

Asteroids ⚳ ⚴ ⚵ ⚶ + 15 new ones for 20th century only 1.00

Astrodynes Power, harmony and discord with summaries for easy comparison 2.00

Chiron, Transpluto or Lilith (only one) in wheel . N/C

Concentric Wheels Any 3 charts available in wheel format may be combined into a '3 wheeler' . 3.00
Deduct $1.00 for each chart ordered as a separate wheel.

Fixed Stars Robson's 110 fixed stars with aspects to natalchart .50

Fortune Finder more Arabic Parts — 97 ancient (Al Biruni) and 99 modern (Robert Hurzt Granite) . 2.00

Graphic Midpoint Sort Proportional spacing highlighs midpt. groupings. **Specify integer divisions of 360°** (1=360°, 4=90°, etc.) 1.00

Harmonic Chart John Addey type. Wheel format, harmonic asc. eq. houses. **Specify harmonic number** . 2.00

Harmonic Positions 30 consecutive sets of positions **Specify starting harmonic number** 1.00

Heliocentric Charts Sun-centered positions . 2.00

House Systems Comparison for 9 systems .50

Local Space Planet compass directions (azimuth & altitude) plus Campanus Mundoscope .50

Locality Map USA, World, Europe, S. Amer., Far East, Austl., Mid East and Africa map showing rise, upper & lower culmination and set lines for each planet . 6.00

Midpoint Structures Midpoint aspects + midpoints in 45° and 90° sequence 1.00

Rectification Assist 10 same-day charts. **Specify starting time, time increment, e.g. 6 am, every 20 minutes** 10.00

Relocation Chart for current location. **Specify original birth data and new location** . 2.00

Uranian Planets + halfsums. .50

Uranian Sensitive Points (includes Uranian Planets). . 3.50

HUMAN RELATIONSHIPS

Chart Comparison (Synastry) All aspects between the two sets of planets plus house positions of one in the other 1.50

Composite Chart Rob Hand-type. Created from midpoints between 2 charts. **Specify location** . 2.00

Relationship Chart Chart erected for space-time midpoint between two births 2.00

COLOR CHARTS

4-Color Wheel any chart we offer in new, aesthetic format with color coded aspect lines. . 2.00

Local Space Map 4-color on 360° circle . 2.00

Custom 6" Disk for any harmonic (laminated, you cut out) overlays on our color wheel charts . 4.00

Plotted Natal Dial for use with custom 6" Disk . 2.00
Specify harmonic #

FUTURE TRENDS

Progressed Chart in wheel format. **Specify progressed day, month and year** . 2.00

Secondary Progressions Day-by-day progressed aspects to natal and progressed planets, ingresses and parallels by month, day and year. **Specify starting year, MC by solar arc (standard) or RA of mean Sun** . 5 years 3.00
10 years 5.00
85 years 15.00

Minor or Tertiary Progressions Minor based on lunar-month-for-a-year, tertiary on day-for-a-lunar-month. **Specify year, MC by solar arc (standard) or RA of mean sun** . 1 year 2.00

Progressed Lifetime Lunar Phases a la Dane Rudhyar . 5.00

Solar Arc Directions Day-by-day solar arc directed aspects to the natal planets, house and sign ingresses by month, day and year. **Specify starting year**. Asc and Vertex arc directions available at same prices 1st 5 years 1.00 Each add'l 5 years .50

Primary Arc Directions (includes speculum) . 5 years 1.50
Specify starting year Each add'l 5 years .50

Transits by all planets except Moon. Date and time of transiting aspects/ingresses to natal chart. **Specify starting month.** Moon-only transits available at same prices. 6 mos. 7.00
OR 12 mos. 12.00
summary only, 6 mos. 3.50
summary only 12 mos. 6.00
calendar (9 planets OR Moon only) 6 mos. 7.00
calendar (9 planets OR Moon only) 12 mos. 12.00
calendar (Moon & planets) 6 mos. 12.00
calendar (Moon & planets) 12 mos. 20.00

Interpretive Transits. SPECIFY STARTING MONTH
Outer Planets ♃♄♅♆♇
Hard Aspects Only ☌☍□∠⚼ 12 MOS. 8.00
Outer Planets ♃♄♅♆♇
Soft & Hard Aspects △✱⚻☌☍□∠⚼ 12 MOS. 10.00
9 Planets ☉☿♀♂♃♄♅♆♇
Hard Aspects Only ☌☍□∠⚼ 6 MOS. 15.00 12 MOS. 25.00
9 Planets ☉☿♀♂♃♄♅♆♇
Soft & Hard Aspects △✱⚻☌☍□∠⚼ 6 MOS. 18.00 12 MOS. 30.00

Returns in wheel format. All returns can be precession corrected. **Specify place, Sun-return year, Moon-return month, planet-return month/year.** . Solar, Lunar or Planet 2.00
13 Lunar 15.00

Custom Graphic Ephemeris in 4 colors. **Specify harmonic, zodiac, starting date.**
1 or 5 YR TRANSITS with or without natal positions . 5.00
1 or 5 YR TRANSITS, NATAL & PROGRESSED 7.00
85 YR PROGRESSIONS with natal positions 10.00
NATAL LINES ONLY (plus transparency) . 4.00
additional natal (same graph) 1.00
additional person's progressions (same graph) . 2.00

POTPOURRI

Winning!! Timing for gamblers, exact planet and transiting house cusps based on Joyce Wehrman's system 1-7 days 3.00
8 or more days 2.00

Biorhythms Chart the 23-day, 28-day and 33-day cycles in black/white graph format. . Printed { per mo. .50 / 12 mos. 4.00 }
4-Color Graph on our plotter Color 6 mos. 2.00

Custom House Cusps Table for each minute of sidereal time. **Specify latitude ° ' "** . 10.00

Custom American Ephemeris Page Any month, 2500BC- AD2500. **Specify zodiac (Sidereal includes RA & dec.)**
One mo. geocentric or two mos. heliocentric . 5.00
One year ephemeris (**specify beginning mo. yr.**) . . 50.00
One year heliocentric ephemeris . . 25.00

Fertility Chart The Jonas method with Sun/Moon-squares/ oppositions to the planets, for 1 year . 3.00
Specify starting month.

Lamination of 1 or 2 sheets 1.00

Transparency (B/W) of any chart or map.
Ordered at same time 1.00

Handling charge per order . 2.00

SAME DAY SERVICE — Ask for Free Catalog

ASTRO COMPUTING SERVICES, Inc.
P.O. BOX 16430
SAN DIEGO, CA 92116-0430
NEIL F. MICHELSEN

(Prices Subject to Change)